INSOLUBLES

Insolubles
Walter Segrave

Critical edition with English translation by Barbara Bartocci and Stephen Read

https://www.openbookpublishers.com

©2024 Barbara Bartocci and Stephen Read

This work is licensed under an Attribution-NonCommercial 4.0 International (CC BY-NC 4.0). This license allows you to share, copy, distribute and transmit the text; to adapt the text for non-commercial purposes of the text providing attribution is made to the authors (but not in any way that suggests that they endorse you or your use of the work). Attribution should include the following information:

Barbara Bartocci and Stephen Read (eds), *Insolubles. Walter Segrave*. Cambridge, UK: Open Book Publishers, 2024, https://doi.org/10.11647/OBP.0359

Further details about CC BY-NC licenses are available at https://creativecommons.org/licenses/by-nc/4.0/

All external links were active at the time of publication unless otherwise stated and have been archived via the Internet Archive Wayback Machine at https://archive.org/web

Digital material and resources associated with this volume are available at https://doi.org/10.11647/OBP.0359#resources

The Medieval Text Consortium Series: Volume 1
ISSN Print: 2754-0634 | ISSN Digital: 2754-0642

ISBN Paperback: 978-1-80511-090-3 | ISBN Hardback: 978-1-80511-091-0 | ISBN Digital (PDF): 978-1-80511-092-7

DOI: 10.11647/OBP.0359

Cover image: Photo by Sean Babbs, 2020, University of Colorado Boulder Libraries Instruction and Outreach | Collections of Distinction Special Collections, Archives, Government Information, and Maps, CC-BY.

Cover design: Jeevanjot Kaur Nagpal

Published by Open Book Publishers in collaboration with Benson Center Press.

EDITORIAL BOARD

Robert Pasnau, *University of Colorado*
Magdalena Bieniak, *University of Warsaw*
Peter Hartman, *Loyola University Chicago*
Peter King, *University of Toronto*
John Marenbon, *University of Cambridge*
Christopher Martin, *University of Auckland*
Giorgio Pini, *Fordham University*
Cecilia Trifogli, *University of Oxford*
Rega Wood, *Indiana University*

Typesetting
Jan Maliszewski, *University of Warsaw*

Table of Contents

Preface ... ix
Introduction ... xi

Conspectus Signorum ... 1

Gualteri Segrave Insolubilia

Capitulum Primum
    De diffinitione insolubilium ... 2
Capitulum Secundum
    Solventes secundum peccatum in materia ... 4
Capitulum Tertium
    Solventes secundum peccatum in forma ... 20
Capitulum Quartum
    Solutio auctoris ... 30
Capitulum Quintum
    Obiectiones contra positionem auctoris et responsiones eiusdem ... 42
Capitulum Sextum
    Solutio insolubilium cathegoricorum et ypotheticorum ... 56
Capitulum Septimum
    De apparentibus insolubilibus ... 100

Bibliography ... 123

Walter Segrave, *Insolubles*

Chapter 1
   Definition of insolubles   3

Chapter 2
   Solutions according to errors in matter   5

Chapter 3
   Solutions according to defects in form   21

Chapter 4
   The author's solution   31

Chapter 5
   Objections to the author's solution and his replies   43

Chapter 6
   Solutions to subject-predicate and compound insolubles   57

Chapter 7
   On merely apparent insolubles   101

A plain text version of the Latin treatise is available from Open Book Publishers.

Preface

Work for the present volume was carried out during a research project funded by the Leverhulme Trust under a Research Project Grant RPG-2016-333 'Theories of Paradox in Fourteenth-Century Logic: Edition and Translation of Key Texts'. We are very grateful to the Trust for their generosity.

We worked through the whole text and translation with members of the Medieval Logic Reading Group at the University of St Andrews during session 2021–22, and learned much from their helpful comments during close line-by-line reading of the text.

Our work was also supported by the University of St Andrews through the School of Philosophical, Anthropological and Film Studies via the Department of Philosophy and the Arché Research Centre for Logic, Language, Metaphysics and Epistemology.

We must also thank the Bodleian Library at the University of Oxford and the Amplonian Library at the University of Erfurt for their assistance in supplying us with copies of the relevant parts of the three extant manuscripts on which this edition is based and for allowing us to publish our research based on these manuscripts.

We would also like to record our gratitude to Jan Maliszewski for his careful work preparing our manuscript and setting it in LaTeX. His thoughtful suggestions for improvements to the presentation of the text were invaluable.

Last, but not least, we are also indebted to the Benson Center at the University of Colorado for its financial support, and to the members of the committee of the Medieval Texts Consortium for their careful reading of the text and translation and their constructive comments and suggestions for improvement. Any remaining errors are of course our own. We hope that the resulting text and translation prove useful to readers and scholars of medieval logic in the future.

Introduction[1]

Walter Segrave's *Insolubles* is a direct response to Thomas Bradwardine's attack on restrictivism (*restrictio*) in his own treatise on insolubles, written in Oxford in the early 1320s.[2] Segrave's treatise must have been composed before 1333, the date of the earliest manuscript in which it is preserved. Walter's text is also, we will see, aware of Kilvington's *Sophismata*, composed at Oxford in the mid-1320s.

According to Emden,[3] Walter de Segrave (or de Sexgrave) was at Merton College, Oxford from 1321 until at least 1338, and had become *Magister Artium* by 1336. The Segrave family, to which Walter may surely have been closely related, was based at Segrave, or Seagrave, in Leicestershire, in the middle of England and as far from the sea as it is possible to be in England, recorded as Setgrave in the Domesday Book of 1085–86. The first Baron de Segrave died in 1295 and Gilbert de Segrave was Bishop of London from 1313 until his death in 1316.[4] From 1340–42 Walter was Chancellor to Richard Aungerville, that is, Richard de Bury, Bishop of Durham, who famously gathered around him some of the very best minds in the kingdom, including Walter Burley, Thomas Bradwardine and Richard Kilvington, all of whom discussed insolubles in their published works. Walter Segrave subsequently became Dean of Chichester, but was dead by 1349.

---

[1] Much of this 'Introduction' is taken from Read, 'Theories of Paradox from Thomas Bradwardine to Paul of Venice', §1 and 'Walter Segrave's "Insolubles": A Restrictivist Response to Bradwardine', §§1–3. (For full bibliographical information on the references, see the Bibliography.)
[2] See Bradwardine, *Insolubilia*, ed. Read, p. 2.
[3] Emden, *A Biographical Register of the University of Oxford to A.D. 1500*, vol. III, col. 1664.
[4] For further information on the de Segrave family, see Segrave, *The Segrave Family 1066–1935*.

1. Insolubles

Although the Liar paradox and similar puzzles were well known and much discussed in antiquity, the medieval interest in them seems to be quite independent and largely in ignorance of those discussions.[5] On the one hand, their paradoxical nature seems not even to have been properly recognised until the end of the twelfth century, and the only reference from antiquity which is regularly cited is Aristotle's discussion of the oath-breaker in his *Sophistical Refutations*, ch. 25. The oath-breaker first says that he will break his oath and then proceeds to fulfil that oath by breaking a subsequent one. To be truly paradoxical, it would need to be one and the same oath which he both fulfils and breaks. This is what we find in the classic case of the Liar paradox, when someone says 'I am lying' (where this is all he says, or at least he means to refer to his own utterance) or 'This utterance is false' (referring to that very utterance). For if it is true then it must be false (for that is what was said), so it is not true (since it cannot be both), and consequently by *reductio ad absurdum* it really is not true, and so is false (assuming it is either true or false, and so if not true, then false). But given, as we have just proved, that it is false, it is surely true (since that is what was said). Thus we have proved both that it is true and that it is false (indeed, that it is both true and not true), and that conclusion is paradoxical (literally, beyond belief). Something has surely gone wrong. It is puzzles like these that the medievals referred to as "insolubles"—not that they are insoluble, but that they are very difficult to solve.[6] But what is the mistake and what is the solution?

2. Cassationism and Restrictivism

We can divide medieval discussions of the insolubles into two main periods, before Bradwardine and after Bradwardine. Thomas Bradwardine wrote his treatise on *Insolubles* in Oxford in the early 1320s and it seems to mark a sea change in the solutions which were mainly favoured. It was standard practice in medieval treatises on insolubles, at least from Bradwardine onwards, to start by describing the faults of rival theories. The dominant theory at the time Bradwardine was writing was restrictivism (*restrictio*), the claim that the part cannot supposit for the whole of which it is part (nor for its contradictory or anything convertible with it), at least in the presence of a privative term, in particular, privative alethic and epistemic terms such as 'false' and 'unknown'.[7] Accordingly, Brad-

---

[5] See, e.g., Spade and Read, 'Insolubles', §2.

[6] See, e.g., Ockham, *Summa Logicae*, ed. Boehner, Gál and Brown, III-3 ch. 46, p. 744: "As for insolubles, you should know that it is not because they can in no way be solved that some sophisms are called insolubles, but because they are solved with difficulty." All translations are our own, unless noted otherwise.

[7] On the medieval notion of supposition and what it is for a term to supposit, see, e.g., Read, 'Medieval Theories of Properties of Terms', §3.

wardine spends two and a half chapters attacking restrictivist theories, leaving only half a chapter to dismiss other solutions before turning to present his own, or as he calls it, "Aristotle's correct solution".

Restrictivism is one of the two types of solution which feature most prominently in discussions of the insolubles before Bradwardine, the other being cassationism (*cassatio*).[8] We know of only two thirteenth-century treatises on insolubles that favour a cassationist solution, according to which those uttering insolubles say nothing at all. For if they did, they would say something true or false, and if so, both—that is, on pain of contradiction. The anonymous author of the *Insolubilia Monacensia* writes:

> An insoluble is a necessary and circular argument to each part of a contradiction [...] For example, that I say a falsehood [...] For that reason, since regarding this utterance it follows, supposing that it is asserted, that it is an insoluble, the response should be 'You say nothing', since generally regarding any utterance everything should be declared void supposing which an insoluble results.[9]

Cassationists are dismissed by Walter Burley, writing at the turn of the fourteenth century, as denying the evidence of their senses, since one only has to listen to Socrates uttering 'Socrates says a falsehood' to hear that he did say something.[10] A cursory glance at Burley's treatise on insolubles might lead one to think that Burley also rejects restrictivism along with cassationism, for Burley follows his rejection of cassationism with a similarly blunt rejection of unqualified restrictivism by observing (Burley, *Insolubilia*, ed. Roure, §2.05) that if Socrates starts to speak by saying 'Something is said by Socrates', he's clearly said something true. But the only thing he said was 'Something is said by Socrates'. So 'something' there must supposit for the whole of which it is part.

But although he rejects unqualified restrictivism, Burley's own solution is a qualified version: no part can supposit for the whole of which it is part when that self-reference (or self-reflection) is accompanied by a privative determination such as 'false' or 'not true':

> Moreover, one should realise that a part never supposits for the whole of which it is part when, putting the whole in the place of the part, what results is reflection of the same on itself with a privative determination. (Burley, *Insolubilia*, §3.03)

---

[8] For a little more detail of cassationism, see Spade and Read, 'Insolubles', §2.5.

[9] De Rijk, 'Some Notes on the Mediaeval Tract De insolubilibus ...', p. 105. De Rijk dubs the treatise "the Munich insolubles" since it survives only in a single manuscript in the Munich Staatsbibliothek. It was written at the end of the twelfth, or more probably at the beginning of the thirteenth century.

[10] See Burley, *Insolubilia*, §2.03: "Furthermore, they deny the evidence of our senses, because they can hear that Socrates says that he says a falsehood, so that Socrates says a falsehood can be said by Socrates."

The reason is, he claims, that everyone saying anything asserts that what he says is true (§3.02), so if anyone says that what he is saying is false he asserts both that it is true and that it is false, and so implicitly asserts a contradiction. Bradwardine, thinking specifically of insolubles, will infer that what was said is false, as is every contradictory utterance. Burley, however, infers the conclusion above, that no part supposits for the whole etc.—he calls it a rule (*regula*). He goes on to illustrate the application of the rule to numerous examples at length.

Bradwardine focusses his criticism on what he calls the "roots" (*radices*) in its "basic assumption" that the part cannot supposit for the whole of which it is part, however qualified:

> Now we could concoct this reason: if the part in such cases did supposit for the whole of which it was part, it would follow that the same proposition was true and false and that insolubles could not possibly be solved. But neither follows, as we will observe in what follows. So this is no more than a concoction of those who do not know how to respond otherwise to the insolubles. (Bradwardine, *Insolubilia*, §3.1.4)

There are many assumptions lying behind the derivation of contradiction in the case of the insolubles, and Bradwardine criticizes restrictivism for giving no reason for singling out self-reference (even self-reference coupled with the presence of a privative term) as the fatal flaw.

3. Bradwardine's Solution

In contrast to Burley's casual and informal presentation of his solution (mainly by example), Bradwardine sets out his assumptions (or postulates) explicitly in order:

> There are six postulates:
>
> (P1) Every proposition is true or false.
>
> (P2) Every proposition signifies or means as a matter of fact or absolutely everything which follows from it as a matter of fact or absolutely ⟨respectively⟩.
>
> (P3) The part can supposit for its whole and for its opposite and for what is equivalent to them.
>
> This postulate, even if it is not immediately obvious, can nonetheless be assumed because it is clear enough from what has gone before.
>
> (P4) Conjunctions and disjunctions with mutually contradictory parts contradict each other.
>
> (P5) From any disjunction together with the opposite of one of its parts the other part may be inferred.

(P6) If a conjunction is true each part is true and conversely; and if it is false, one of its parts is false and conversely. And if a disjunction is true, one of its parts is true and conversely; and if it is false, each part is false and conversely. (Bradwardine, *Insolubilia*, §6.3)

The third postulate affirms Bradwardine's rejection of restrictivism. The second postulate is what is most distinctive of his solution. Behind it lies Bradwardine's fundamental idea, namely, that propositions may, indeed do mean more than at first appears. This claim became the main battleground in debates about insolubles for the rest of the fourteenth century, and beyond. It was not completely novel, for as we have seen, Burley himself claimed that anyone saying anything implicitly asserts that what they say is true, an idea going back at least to Bonaventure—indeed, according to Segrave to Aristotle.[11] But Bradwardine took it further, and (P2) is at once a control and a generator of what lies hidden in a proposition. He also, in modern parlance, moved that hidden component from illocutionary force (assertion) to locutionary meaning (signification). Very many subsequent proposals about the insolubles, those of William Heytesbury, Gregory of Rimini, John Buridan, Albert of Saxony, Peter of Ailly, Marsilius of Inghen, Robert Eland, Ralph Strode, John of Holland and John Hunter, both at Oxford and at Paris, turned on the existence of such tacit or implicit signification. Few stood out against it, notably Roger Swyneshed and his followers.

On all the other postulates, including (P1), Bradwardine and Burley agree. For every insoluble is either affirmative or negative, says Burley,[12] and every affirmative insoluble is false and every negative insoluble is true, he says—but here Bradwardine differs: for him, every insoluble is false. Burley does not spell out his account of truth and falsehood here, but he does elsewhere. Conti ('Walter Burley', §2) notes that "the three main principles of his semantic theory remained the same throughout his academic career", the third being that a proposition "is true if and only if it is the sign of 'the truth of things' (*veritas rerum*)." In general, Burley's account was that truth is the adequation of thought and reality (Conti, *ibid.*, §5), but more practically, the true propositions correspond to real propositions composed of the significates of their constituent terms together with a copula of identity, so that an affirmative subject-predicate proposition is true if and only if the significates are identical (*ibid.*, §5). But given his extended notion of signification, Bradwardine has to modify the account of truth. Accordingly, he defines a true proposition as an utterance signifying only as things are and a false proposition as an utterance signifying other than things are (Bradwardine, *Insolubilia*, §6.4):

The definitions are two, of which the first is this:

---

[11] See §5 below and §4.5 in Segrave's text. See also Spade and Read, 'Insolubles', §3.5.
[12] Burley, *Insolubilia*, §3.05, and Bradwardine agrees: *Insolubilia*, §6.1.

(D1) A true proposition is an utterance signifying only as things are. The second is this:

(D2) A false proposition is an utterance signifying other than things are. (Bradwardine, *Insolubilia*, §6.2)

From these definitions, together with the six postulates, he is able to prove his main conclusion:

> If any proposition signifies itself not to be true or itself to be false, it signifies itself to be true and is false.

Note that the claim is restricted to propositions which signify themselves not to be true or to be false, that is, to insolubles. Bradwardine does not simply claim or postulate this. He proves, by an elaborate argument which deserves close analysis (Bradwardine, *Insolubilia*, §§6.5.1–6.5.2), that all insolubles signify of themselves that they are true. Suppose that all I say is 'I am not speaking the truth' (*ego non dico verum*), for example. By Bradwardine's main conclusion this signifies not only that I am not speaking the truth, and so that it itself is not true (by P2, since it is the only thing I say), but also that it is true. So things cannot be wholly as it signifies, since it cannot be both true and not true. Hence, Bradwardine concludes, what I said was false.

Not so for Burley, as he spells out at length:

> If anyone begins to speak like this: 'I am not speaking the truth', then this is true. (Burley, *Insolubilia*, §3.05)

For 'truth' in that utterance cannot supposit for the whole of which it is part. It must supposit either for some other utterance of mine, or for nothing. But there was no other utterance of mine. So 'truth' here lacks a suppositum. Now as a general rule, the medievals took existential import seriously. Affirmatives with empty terms are false, and correspondingly, negative propositions with empty terms are true.[13] So for Burley, my utterance is true.

4. The Structure of Segrave's Treatise

Segrave's treatise runs to some 13400 words, the English translation to some 18000 words. It is divided in the Erfurt manuscript Octavo 76 (siglum: E_8) into seven chapters. The first chapter briefly defines what Segrave takes to be the essential nature of an insoluble, which will be

---

[13] See, e.g., Klima, 'Existence and Reference in Medieval Logic', p. 198.

fully elaborated in the fourth chapter. The second and third chapters argue against previous solutions, which Segrave divides into two main groups: those which claim that insolubles are paralogisms defective in their matter, on the one hand; and those identifying an error in their form, on the other hand. In the second chapter, which presents solutions based on errors in matter, Segrave lists the cassationists, who are dismissed rapidly, and those who, like Bradwardine, claim that insolubles are self-contradictory in signifying themselves not only to be false but also to be true (see §2.2.1). In the third chapter, Segrave argues against solutions which identify the error in the paralogisms' form (*peccantia in forma*), namely, those which appeal in one way or another to the fallacy of the conditional and the unconditional (*fallacia secundum quid et simpliciter*).

The fourth chapter presents Segrave's own solution in detail. Unlike previous forms of the restrictivist solution, which Bradwardine divides into those appealing to the fallacy of the conditional and the unconditional, those solving insolubles by the fallacy of form of expression (*forma dictionis*), those appealing to the fallacy of false cause (*non causa ut causa*) and those restricting the time rather than the reference (*suppositio*), Segrave identifies a fallacy of accident in them (see §6 below). In the fifth chapter he considers a number of objections, in the sixth he illustrates his solution by applying it to a wide range of familiar and less familiar examples (including Kilvington's notorious 48th sophism),[14] and in the final chapter he discusses sophisms which only seem to be insolubles but in fact are not.

5. *Obligationes*

There is much use in Segrave's treatise, as in most other fourteenth-century treatises on insolubles, of the language of *obligationes*, logical obligations. This is a sui generis species of logical activity, consisting of a unique kind of dialogue between an Opponent and a Respondent governed by strict rules. Starting in the thirteenth century, several species of *obligatio* were distinguished, the main one being *positio*. A *positio* opens with the description by the Opponent of a background scenario, and the positing of a proposition, known therefore as the *positum*. That proposition is usually, though not necessarily, one which is false in the scenario, and the *positio* should be admitted by the Respondent if (and only if) the scenario and *positum* are (or at least could be) possible. Further propositions are then presented to the Respondent, who is required to grant, deny or doubt (or at least, "express doubt about") them in line with the following rules (which vary in detail between different authors):

---

[14] See §6.14 in Segrave's text, and B. and N. Kretzmann (eds), *The Sophismata of Richard Kilvington*, Sophism 48.

— If the proposition follows from or is inconsistent with the *positum* (and what has earlier been granted and the opposite of what has been denied), it is deemed relevant, and must be granted if it follows and denied if inconsistent;

— otherwise it is irrelevant, and should be granted if known to be true in the scenario specified, denied if known to be false, and doubted if its truth-value is unknown.

In general, the Respondent can in principle follow these rules without contradicting himself; but he responds badly if he grants contradictory propositions or grants and denies the same proposition. A proposition is deemed to have been granted if its contradictory has been denied, and vice versa. After a specified time, or when it is thought that the Respondent has responded badly, the *obligatio* is paused or terminated (*Cedat tempus*) and the Respondent's responses are analysed.

Several of the paralogisms in ch. 6 are given explicitly in the form of an *obligatio*. Take, for example, the insoluble presented in §6.6: the scenario is that A is either 'God exists' or 'Nothing proposed to Socrates should be granted by you', you don't know which; and it is posited that 'A is true' is the only proposition proposed to Socrates. Then 'A is true' is proposed to you. Should you grant, deny or doubt it? This is about as far as the obligation itself gets. What we're presented with over the next couple of pages is, first, an insoluble: you can't deny it, you can't doubt it, but it seems you can't grant it either. Segrave's resolution is to show that, although 'A is true' should be granted, A itself should be doubted, that is, you know A is true even though you don't know what A says.[15] (A non-insoluble example might be one where you know A is either 'God exists' or 'A man is not a donkey': you don't know what A is, or says, but at least you know it's true, whichever it is.) The argument against granting 'A is true' turns on the apparent self-reference in A: since 'A is true' is the only proposition proposed to Socrates, if A is 'Nothing proposed to Socrates should be granted by you', A will be equivalent to '"A is true" should not be granted by you', preventing you from granting it on pain of contradicting the *positum*. Segrave's solution to the insolubles claims that this equivalence fails, dissolving the paradox.

Further examples concerning whether or not to grant what is proposed to you are found in §§6.7, 6.10, 6.11, 6.12 and 6.13. A particularly elaborate obligation is found in §6.14. However, there are other uses of forms of the verb 'ponere' and the corresponding noun 'positio' which should not be taken in the technical sense associated with obligations. For example, when Segrave writes (§ad 2.1.1): "Sed ista positio negat sensum", he

---

[15] Similar puzzles about whether one can doubt what one knows are discussed by Heytesbury in his 'De Scire': see Heytesbury, 'The Verbs "Know" and "Doubt"'.

is not referring to an obligational positio, but to the solution (that is, proposed solution) or opinion or claim of the cassationists. Similarly, at §2.2.1 ("Ratio autem istius positionis") he is referring to Bradwardine's proposed solution, and repeatedly in the paragraphs that follow. Again, in §2.1.1 Segrave introduces the classic Liar Paradox: 'Ego dico falsum' ('I say a falsehood') as uttered by Socrates, with the phrase 'ponatur', and in the following paragraph refers back to it: 'casu posito' ('in the scenario proposed'). This is no more than familiar use of 'ponere' and its cognate forms ('supponere', 'proponere') to describe the act of supposing, or claiming, or proposing. It is important to recognise that many of the medievals' technical terms also enjoy a familiar and non-technical usage.

6. Segrave's Solution

Like Burley, Segrave shares many assumptions with Bradwardine, apart of course from (P3). Indeed, at a couple of points Segrave appears to endorse Bradwardine's second postulate (P2), that a proposition signifies everything implied by what it signifies.[16] For the heart of Segrave's solution is that, since (as we saw Burley and Bonaventure claim) whoever asserts a proposition asserts that it is true, the restriction on supposition that Segrave maintains is that:

> The extremes of a proposition only supposit ⟨for⟩ those things about which the whole can mean that it itself is true, assuming that it exists, and those extremes do not supposit ⟨for⟩ those things about which the whole, assuming that it exists, would mean that it itself is false. And this is what I claim. (§4.5.3)

The reason Segrave gives is that:

> it is because the extremes take their supposition from the copula, whose significate is that the proposition is true, as was said. So the extreme does not supposit for anything about which the whole would mean that it itself is false or is not true, because this would be inconsistent with the significate of the copula, and so the extremes should be restricted by the meaning of the copula. (§ad 4.6.2)

Consider, e.g., he says

> A falsehood exists,

---

[16] This is to interpret (P2) as a closure postulate: see, e.g., Bradwardine, *Insolubilia*, 'Introduction', p. 17. However, there is an alternative interpretation, found in Paul of Venice's *Logica Magna*: see Read, 'Truth, Signification and Paradox', p. 405.

call it A, and suppose there is no other falsehood—perhaps God has annihilated all other propositions, or all other existential propositions.

> But it is evident that this:
>> A falsehood exists,
>
> does not signify that no other falsehood exists. For it always signifies in one way for its own part, since it does not have a mind of its own [...] But on the contrary: this inference is necessary:
>> A is false, therefore no other falsehood than A exists,
>
> because if there were another falsehood, then A would be true, so whatever implies or signifies the premise signifies the conclusion, so from the opposite, the premise does not signify what the conclusion does not signify. (§§ad 4.6 – ad 4.6.1)

According to Bradwardine, A signifies that A is false, since that follows *ut nunc* (as a matter of fact, given that no other falsehood exists) from A—or rather, from what A signifies, namely, that a falsehood exists. But if A is false then no other falsehood exists, for, Segrave observes, if there were another falsehood, A would be true. So, by Bradwardine's second postulate (P2), since A signifies that A is false, it signifies that no other falsehood exists. But we agreed that A does not signify that, so it follows that it does not signify that it itself is false, either.

One might wonder if Segrave is really endorsing and using Bradwardine's postulate (P2) in his own person here. For this would seem to be an argument against Bradwardine, and so arguably simply *ad hominem*. But Segrave also appeals to (P2) a little earlier in providing justification for Burley's claim that every proposition signifies (or at least, for Burley, asserts) its own truth. Recall that Bradwardine's main conclusion applies only to insolubles, that is, propositions signifying their own falsehood. Segrave bases his stronger claim on the role of the copula, referring to Aristotle's remark that "the 'is' in a statement also means that the statement is true and 'is not' that it is not true" and Averroes' comment that "'being' here signifies nothing but truth."[17] From this, Segrave draws his only postulate:

> The postulate is this: that every proposition means things being in reality as it signifies. This is self-evident and is clear from the Philosopher and the Commentator in comment 14 on the fifth book of the *Metaphysics* and throughout the text of that comment: for the copula in the proposition signifies being true, as is elucidated there [...]
>
> From this what was claimed follows ostensively in this way: every proposition not involving a contradiction signifies things being in reality as it signifies, and does not signify things not being ⟨in reality as it signifies⟩. But things

---

[17] Aristotle, *Metaphysics*, tr. Hope, Δ 7, 1017a30; Averroes, *In Metaphysicen* (ed. Venice, f. 117E, https://archive.org/details/bub_gb_u_T0u0IuuyIC/page/n251/mode/2up; ed. Ponzalli, pp. 131–32): "*universaliter hoc nomen ens hic non significat nisi verum.*"

being in reality as the proposition signifies, and not things not being (in
reality as it signifies) is for a proposition to be true and not false, provided
the proposition exists; so every proposition not involving a contradiction,
assuming it exists, signifies itself to be true and not false. (§§4.5–4.5.2)

Segrave takes an example: suppose you are sitting.

> [...] this inference is valid:
>> Things are in reality wholly as the proposition 'You are sitting' signifies,
>> and it exists, therefore this proposition is true and not false,
>
> and the same is true of other propositions. Therefore, every proposition not
> involving a contradiction, assuming it exists, signifies itself to be true and not
> false. (§4.5.2)

The caveat "assuming it exists" reflects the fact that the medievals took propositions to be concrete, individual utterances which could not be true or false unless they actually existed. What is striking is that Segrave, taking 'You are sitting' as an arbitrary example, and generalizing it to represent any proposition, infers that any such non-contradictory proposition signifies itself to be true and not false. He is here clearly appealing to Bradwardine's second postulate, that signification is closed under implication, so if from any non-contradictory proposition it follows that it is true and not false, then that is part of what it signifies.

7. The Fallacy of Accident

Burley and Bradwardine agree on one thing: that insolubles commit the fallacy of the conditional and the unconditional (*simpliciter et secundum quid*), taking this from Aristotle's treatment in his *De Sophisticis Elenchis* of the example of the man who swears that he is forsworn.[18] Segrave says they are mistaken: according to him, insolubles commit the fallacy of accident.

The fallacy of accident is the first of the fallacies described by Aristotle in *De Sophisticis Elenchis* as those "independent of language", and discussed at some length in ch. 24. The classic example is the Hidden Man puzzle: you know your father (or Coriscus), your father (or Coriscus) is the man approaching, but you don't know the man approaching (since he is wearing a mask, or too far away to recognise, etc.). Aristotle's diagnosis was that one or more of the two properties attached to Coriscus (being known by you and being the man approaching) is accidental (or incidental) to him and so there is no essential connection to support the necessity required correctly to infer the conclusion from the premises.

---

[18] Aristotle, *De Sophisticis Elenchis*, ch. 25; Burley, *Insolubilia*, §4.05 (cf. Bradwardine, *Insolubilia*, §3.0); Bradwardine, *Insolubilia*, §§7.11–7.11.3 (and 'Introduction', p. 6).

It has to be said that Aristotle's discussion of the fallacy of accident is neither clear nor convincing. What he says about examples such as the Hidden Man appears to clash with the principle of expository syllogism (or *ecthesis*), stated in *De Sophisticis Elenchis*,[19] and arguably invoked by Aristotle in *Prior Analytics* to give an alternative proof of Darapti:

> The demonstration ⟨of Darapti⟩ can also be carried out *per impossibile* [i.e., by indirect reduction] or by *ecthesis* [i.e. setting out]. For if both terms belong to all S and one chooses one of the Ss, say N, then both P and R will belong to it, so that P will belong to some R.[20]

Buridan claims, pace Aristotle, that expository syllogism is the real basis of the syllogism (not the *dici de omni et nullo*):

> Every affirmative syllogism holds by virtue of the principle 'what things are said to be universally identical with one and the same thing are also said to be identical between themselves',[21]

that is, the very principle Aristotle states in ch. 6 of *De Sophisticis Elenchis*, and negative syllogisms by a corresponding principle of difference. Yet the Hidden Man can be put in exactly the form Aristotle describes as *ecthesis*:

> Being known by you is said of Coriscus
> Being the man approaching is said of Coriscus
> So being known by you is said of the man approaching.

How then can the premises be true and the conclusion false?[22]

One medieval attempt to clarify the fallacy of accident so as to accord with Aristotle's theory of the syllogism is found in Giles of Rome. The fallacy arises, he said, when there is a variation in the supposition of the middle term:

> That the major term, if it is true of the middle term, must then be true of the minor term, only happens in the case of those middle terms which are indifferent according to substance, because it requires the middle term not to vary or be diverse if the conclusion is to follow of necessity.[23]

---

[19] Aristotle, *De Sophisticis Elenchis*, ch. 6, 168b32: "we claim that things that are the same as one and the same thing are also the same as each other."

[20] Aristotle, *Prior Analytics* I 6, 28a24–26.

[21] Buridan, *Summulae de Dialectica*, tr. Klima, §5.1.8, p. 313. See also Buridan, *Treatise on Consequences*, tr. Read, III I 4 and 'Introduction', p. 22.

[22] Aristotle's remarks on the fallacy of accident also appear to conflict with the dici de omni. See Gelber, 'The Fallacy of Accident and the "dictum de omni"', §I, where she discusses how Boethius and others tried to reconcile this conflict.

[23] Aegidius Romanus, *Expositio supra libros Elenchorum*, cited in Ockham, *Expositio super libros Elenchorum*, ed. Del Punta, II ch. 9 §2, pp. 230–31.

Giles attempts to square this with what Aristotle says in *De Sophisticis Elenchis*:

> It should be said that it is not Aristotle's intention to deny that in no way are the unknown and the known the same; but he means that this fallacy is almost argued in four terms and always has diversity of middle term; so he says that the same is not known and unknown, because 'Coriscus' is used in different ways and almost has the power of two terms, as he is placed with respect to knowledge and as he is approaching.[24]

Burley extends the idea of variation of the supposition of terms to the extremes:

> In this fallacy there should be assigned three, namely, the attribute, the accident and the subject thing. And according to Giles, the major extreme is always the attribute and the middle term the subject thing and the minor extreme the accident. But this is not a big worry, for it suffices for there to be this fallacy that some term is not included but is compared to two other terms in the argument. Whence it should be realised that the fallacy of accident sometimes results from a variation of the middle term and sometimes from a variation of the major or minor extreme.[25]

It is not quite so straightforward, says Burley, to identify the fallacy in the Hidden Man puzzle:

> According to this fallacy, the paralogism is given in this way:
>
> The one coming is known by you, Coriscus is the one coming, hence etc.
>
> Or like this:
>
> Coriscus is known by you and is the one coming, hence etc.
>
> And it is usually said that it is a fallacy of accident from the variation of this term 'Coriscus', for concerning Coriscus in that he is known by you it is not included that he is the one coming. But on the contrary: it seems that this is not a fallacy. For from the opposite of the consequent we may with the minor premise infer syllogistically the opposite of the major premise. For this syllogism is correct:
>
> No one coming is known by you, Coriscus is the one coming, hence etc.
>
> Then it seems that in the first argument there is no fallacy of accident in respect of this conclusion, 'the one coming is known by you', and Aristotle understood this, but it is a fallacy of accident in respect of the reduplicative conclusion, or in respect of this conclusion, 'the one coming insofar as he is coming is known by you', and then it is not a fallacy of accident from the variation of the middle term, but from the variation of the minor extreme, because this term 'the one coming' is taken in different ways in the minor premise and in the conclusion.[26]

---

[24] Aegidius Romanus, *Expositio supra libros Elenchorum*, cited in Ockham, *ibid.*, II ch. 9 §2, p. 231 n. 3.

[25] Walter Burley, *Tractatus super librum Elenchorum*, cited in Ockham, *loc. cit.* This work may have been written at Oxford before Burley left for Paris in around 1307: see Ottman and Wood, 'Walter of Burley', p. 7.

[26] Burley, *loc. cit.*, cited in Ockham, *Expositio super libros Elenchorum*, II ch. 9 §2, p. 232 n. 4.

Typical cases of reduplication employ the expressions 'qua' or 'insofar as', e.g., 'I know Coriscus qua the one approaching'. The medievals often used reduplication as a test for whether the fallacy of accident was present.[27] So, e.g., Ockham complains that it is commonly said that the Hidden Man paralogism is shown to commit a fallacy of accident since "it is not included that Coriscus is approaching insofar as he is known ⟨by you⟩." (Ockham, *ibid.*, pp. 231–2)

Segrave spells this out in response to the objection that Aristotle does not seem to attribute the fallacy of accident to insolubles:

> Finally, ⟨one can argue⟩ like this: if these paralogisms were to be solved by the fallacy of accident, then since it not likely that they passed unnoticed by Aristotle, he would have solved such paralogisms, where he does solve them, by the fallacy of accident. (§5.9)

Segrave responds:

> To the final argument: I say that where Aristotle solves the paralogisms by the fallacy of accident, he shows how to solve paralogisms of this kind, because they have the same defect, as was proved before ⟨in ch. 4⟩. For in insolubles the supposition of the middle or extreme term always varies; and this is to commit the fallacy of accident. Thus these paralogisms are similar to insolubles in which, since the middle term is a this-something, the extremes are not connected. For one argues like this in insolubles, just as here:
>
>> Coriscus is known by you, Coriscus is approaching, therefore the one who is approaching is known by you,
>
> for the term 'approaching' is taken, or at least should be understood, reduplicatively, and so the supposition of the extreme varies. (§ad 5.9)

Segrave recognises that to diagnose a fallacy or paralogism one needs not only to show that the reasoning involved is invalid; one must also show why it appears to be valid and so tempts people to commit the fallacy. Insolubles are so called, he says, not because it is impossible to solve them, but because solving them is difficult. Once again, he is here in agreement with Ockham and Bradwardine.[28] But he goes on to claim that insolubles are particularly difficult to solve since "having filled in the additional premises from which they derive their evidential force, they seem not to differ in any way from good syllogisms":

> For they have the same syntactic arrangement both in mood and figure, e.g.,
>
>> No falsehood is said by Socrates, this is a falsehood, so this is not said by Socrates.
>
> Therefore, since ⟨insolubles⟩ have the greatest causes of appearing ⟨to be good syllogisms⟩, which are just the same as those of a good syllogism, for

---

[27] See, e.g., Gelber, 'The Fallacy of Accident', §IV.
[28] See §1 above, and Bradwardine, *Insolubilia*, §2.1.

this reason they are the most difficult to solve. Hence they are deservedly called insolubles *par excellence* because of their outstanding argumentative strength. (§1.1)

He explains:

⟨An insoluble⟩ commits the fallacy of accident because by arguing like this:

This is said by Socrates and this is a falsehood, so a falsehood is said by Socrates,

the term 'falsehood' supposits in the minor premise for something it does not supposit for in the conclusion. Similarly, in arguing like this:

No falsehood is said by Socrates, this is a falsehood, so this is not said by Socrates,

there is a variation in the middle term because the term 'falsehood' supposits for one thing in the major premise and another in the minor, according to those advocating this solution. And thus it is clear that they have to solve these kinds of paralogisms according to the fallacy of accident, namely, from a variation of the middle term or of an extreme term. (§3.4)

Segrave supports this diagnosis with a brief discussion of supposition theory. Terms only have supposition in the context of a proposition, and (except in material supposition) supposit for what they signify—but often not for all their significates. For example, in

A rational animal is a man

'animal' supposits only for men, not for all animals, because its range of supposition is restricted by adjoining the expression 'rational'. Indeed,

To supposit for its supposita is to signify them to be the extremes of that union in reality which the copula signifies. They do this sometimes conjunctively, sometimes disjunctively, insofar as they receive a different mode of suppositing from what is adjoined to them. (§4.4)

The ground has now been laid for Segrave to solve the insolubles by the fallacy of accident. He illustrates his solution in part by responding directly to Bradwardine's extensive arguments against restrictivism.

8. The Manuscripts and the Edition

Segrave's treatise is preserved in three manuscripts, although one of these is acephalic and contains only half of the treatise:

E_4 = Erfurt, Universitäts- und Forschungsbibliothek Erfurt/Gotha, UB Erfurt, Codices Amploniani 4° 276, ff. 159ra–162ra, cursive hand. This manuscript contains a collection of logical works, including chapters 6–12 of Bradwardine's *Insolubilia*.[29]

E_8 = Erfurt, Universitäts- und Forschungsbibliothek Erfurt/Gotha, UB Erfurt, Codices Amploniani 8° 76, ff. 21vb–34rb, mid-fourteenth century(?), Anglican hand. This manuscript contains other logical treatises (e.g., Bradwardine's *Insolubilia*) and physical writings by Walter Burley.[30]

O = Oxford, Bodleian Library, Canon. Misc. 219, ff. 1r–3r (acephalic, the text starting at the end of §ad 5.2). This manuscript dates from the end of the fourteenth century and consists of three parts;[31] the first part contains Segrave's insolubles along with Bradwardine's and the so-called Pseudo-Heytesbury's.[32]

We have established the Latin text using all three manuscripts; we have generally followed the readings of E_8, except where the readings of either or both E_4 and O were clearly preferable, for E_8 generally presents fewer obvious errors. In a few places, where all the manuscripts had mistaken (or apparently mistaken) readings, we have emended the text and listed the readings of the manuscripts in the critical apparatus. The critical apparatus records relevant variants, such as multiple- and single-word omissions, and also inversions of words or phrases. We have not noted the recurring cases in which one or two manuscripts have *ille* and the other(s) *iste* or vice versa, or where one or two manuscripts have *igitur* and the other(s) *ergo* and vice versa, nor differences in spelling between the manuscripts or what we thought were irrelevant scribal corrections. We have preferred to adopt the medieval manuscript spellings, including *e* for *ae*, and *Sortes* and *periurius* for *Socrates* and *periurus*. We have adopted modern (English) punctuation as the meaning of the text requires. The section headings and division into paragraphs are ours.

In translating the text, we have tried to stay as close as possible to the Latin text and to be as consistent as possible. In some cases, we have inserted words in ⟨angle brackets⟩ in order to make the translation more explicit and clearer.

---

[29] See W. Schum, *Beschreibendes Verzeichniss*, pp. 517–19.

[30] Digital facsimile of E_8 is available at: https://dhb.thulb.uni-jena.de/rsc/viewer/ufb_derivate_00016465/CA-8-00076_0048.tif. Pagination markers in the digital version of this edition provide links to the individual folios.

[31] A. Maierù, 'Le Ms. Oxford, Canonici misc. 219 et la "Logica" de Strode', pp. 98–103.

[32] The author of this anonymous treatise was dubbed "pseudo-Heytesbury" by Spade (*The Medieval Liar*, p. 35) because his treatise is so closely modelled on that of Heytesbury. See also Read, 'Theories of Paradox from Thomas Bradwardine to Paul of Venice', §4.

Conspectus Signorum

In textu latino et anglico

⟨ ⟩ = uncis acutis indicantur litterae vel verba ab editoribus addita

[ ] = uncis angulatis indicantur verba ab editoribus deleta

In apparatu critico

α ... β = omnia verba ab α usque ad β (e.g.: *dicit ... falsum* = a verbo *dicit* usque ad verbum *falsum*)

Conspectus abbreviationum in apparatu critico

a.c. = *ante correctionem*
add. = *addidit, -erunt*
corr. = *correximus*
del. = *delevit, -erunt*
dub. = *dubitanter*
exp. = *expunctus est*
fol., fols. = *folium, folia*
inv. = *invertit, -erunt*
(in) marg. = *in margine*
iter. = *iteravit, -erunt*
mss. = *codices*
om. = *omisit, -erunt*
om. (hom.) = *omisit, -erunt (per homoeoteleuton)*
p.c. = *post correctionem*
scr. = *scripsit, -erunt*

⟨Gualteri Segrave Insolubilia⟩

0.1 | Sicut vult philosophus 2° Metaphysice, non solum debemus grates reddere hiis qui nobiscum in opinionibus conveniunt, sed et hiis qui a nobis dissonant nostrasque opiniones inpugnant. Tales namque, etsi a via veritatis frequenter exorbitent, alios tamen ad hoc excitant ut vel illam adhuc inveniendam inquirant vel ut firmius roborent iam inventam. Quia igitur circa solutionem sophysmatum insolubilium diversi diversas scripserunt sententias sibi invicem repugnantes, quorumdam coactus rogatione illas duxi summarie recitandas ut sic pensatis hinc inde rationibus antiqua veritas plenius elucescat, a qua multum recedere non intendo, cum non sit verisimile illam sententiam fore penitus reprobandam quam tot et tanti inquisicione super hac habita diligenti diutius comprobaverunt.

Capitulum Primum
⟨De diffinitione insolubilium⟩

1.0 | Insolubile ergo de quo presens versatur intentio non dicitur quia ipsum solvi est impossibile sed quia illud solvere est difficile; nec omne tale est insolubile, sed illi soli paralogismi dicuntur insolubiles ubi ex singulari infertur sua particularis secundum vocem vel ex universali sua singularis secundum vocem.

Et voco singularem secundum vocem alicuius propositionis que cum illa convenit in subiecto et predicato ut:

> Hoc falsum dicitur a Sorte,

est singulare secundum vocem huius particularis:

> Falsum dicitur a Sorte.

1.1 Nec mirum si tales paralogismi merito dicuntur insolubiles. Expletis enim mediis a quibus capiunt evidentiam, a bonis sillogismis nullatenus

---

2 conveniunt] sunt (*dub.*) E_4 4 ad hoc] adhuc E_8 5 adhuc] ad hoc E_4 6 diversas] diversa E_8 8 summarie] super mane E_4 || inde] *om.* E_4 9 plenius] *add. in marg. eadem manus* E_4 10 illam] idem E_4 11 hac] hanc E_4 *ante* (*dub.*) *add.* E_4 12 Capitulum Primum] *in marg.* E_8 16 soli] sillogismi (*dub.*) E_4 17 sua²] *iter.* E_8 20 convenit] conveniat E_8 || ut] et E_4

⟨Walter Segrave, *Insolubles*⟩

0.1 As Aristotle recommends in *Metaphysics* 2,[1] we should give thanks not only to those who agree with our opinions, but also to those who disagree with us and criticize our opinions.[2] For even if ⟨the latter⟩ often stray from the path of truth, they nonetheless inspire others either to seek the truth yet to be found or to confirm more resolutely that truth which they have found. Hence, because different people have written different mutually inconsistent things about the solution to insoluble sophisms, I was induced by requests from some people to rehearse the chief points, so that, once the reasons having been weighed on each side, the old truth will shine forth more fully.[3] I do not intend to depart much from that truth, since it is unlikely that an opinion which so many people have advocated for so long with such diligent enquiry should be completely rejected.

Chapter 1
⟨Definition of insolubles⟩

1.0 An insoluble, which is our present concern, is not so called because it is impossible to solve, but because solving it is difficult. Nor is everything like that an insoluble, but only those paralogisms are called insolubles where from a singular proposition a syntactic particular of it is inferred or from a universal proposition a syntactic singular of it.

I say that a syntactic singular of some proposition is ⟨any singular proposition⟩ which has the same subject and predicate, e.g.,

> This falsehood is said by Socrates

is a syntactic singular of this particular proposition:

> A falsehood is said by Socrates.

1.1 Nor is it surprising that such paralogisms are correctly called insolubles. For having filled in the additional premises from which they

---

[1] *Metaphysics* α, 993b12.
[2] See Hamesse, *Les Auctoritates Aristotelis*, p. 118 #36 (Non solum his dicere gratias justum est quorum opinionibus aliquis communicavit, sed etiam qui superficialiter enuntiarunt, quia hi etiam conferunt aliquid) and Averroes, *In II Metaphysicen* (in Averroes, *Aristotelis Metaphysicorum libri XIIII cum Averrois Commentariis*), comm. 2, f. 29F (https://archive.org/details/bub_gb_u_T0u0IuuyIC/page/n65/mode/2up).
[3] By "the old truth" (*antiqua veritas*), Segrave is alluding to what before Bradwardine's attacks on it had been the standard solution to the insolubles, namely, restrictivism. See 'Introduction', §2.

differre videntur. Habent enim secundum vocem dispositionem tam modi quam figure, ut hic:

> Nullum falsum dicitur a Sorte, hoc est falsum, ergo hoc non dicitur a Sorte.

Tales igitur, quia causas apparentie habent maximas quoniam easdem quas et boni sillogismi, ideo ad solvendum sunt difficillimi. Merito ergo anthonomastice per earum maximam evidenciam insolubilia nuncupantur.

1.2 Visa igitur talium paralogismorum apparentia iam restat eorumdem non existentiam explicare. Pro quo sciendum quod quidam ponunt illos deficere in materia, quidam in forma.

Capitulum Secundum
⟨Solventes secundum peccatum in materia: cassantes⟩

2.1 Ponentes defectum in materia sunt bipartiti: quidam dicunt quodlibet insolubile oriri ex actu nostro aliquo, cuiusmodi sunt intelligere, cognoscere, scribere et huiusmodi; et illos actus in solvendo negant, et hii dicuntur cassantes.

2.1.1 Verbi gratia, ponatur Sortem dicere:

> Ego dico falsum,

et arguitur sic: Sortes dicit aliquid, aut ergo falsum vel verum. Si verum, ergo verum est Sortem dicere falsum, ergo | dicit falsum. Si falsum, ergo falsum est Sortem dicere falsum, ergo non dicit falsum. Respondent hii quod Sortes nihil dicit nec loquitur, et ita interimunt actus dicendi.

E_8 22rb

2.1.2 Istorum ratio potissima est hec: casu posito, dicunt ipsi:

> Hec est falsa: Sortes dicit falsum,

---

1 differre] differit E_4 ‖ vocem] voces E_8 6 ideo] *add. in marg.* E_4 7 per] pro E_4 ‖ evidenciam *corr.*] evidencia *mss*   10 illos] eos E_4 12 Capitulum Secundum] *in marg.* E_8 14 quidam] enim *add.* E_4 16 solvendo] solvere *a.c.* E_8 solvere res E_4 20 falsum ... verum] *inv.* E_4 23 nihil] nec E_8

derive their evidential force, they seem not to differ in any way from good syllogisms. For they have the same syntactic arrangement both in mood and figure, e.g.,

> No falsehood is said by Socrates, this is a falsehood, so this is not said by Socrates.

Therefore, since ⟨insolubles⟩ have the greatest causes of appearing ⟨to be good syllogisms⟩, which are just the same as those of a good syllogism, for this reason they are the most difficult to solve. Hence they are deservedly called insolubles *par excellence* because of their outstanding argumentative strength.

1.2 Having seen ⟨why⟩ these paralogisms appear ⟨to be good syllogisms⟩, it now remains to explain their not being ⟨good syllogisms⟩. To this end, it should be noted that some people propose a defect in matter, others a defect in form.[4]

Chapter 2
⟨Solutions according to errors in matter: cassationists⟩

2.1 Those proposing a defect in matter are of two kinds: for some say that every insoluble arises from some act of ours such as understanding, knowing, writing and suchlike; and they deny ⟨the existence of⟩ these acts in their solution and they are called Cassationists.[5]

2.1.1 For example, suppose Socrates says:

> I say a falsehood

and one argues like this: Socrates says something, so ⟨he says⟩ either a falsehood or a truth. If a truth, then it is true that Socrates says a falsehood, so he says a falsehood. If a falsehood, then it is false that Socrates says a falsehood, so he does not say a falsehood. Cassationists respond that Socrates says nothing nor does he speak, and so they nullify the act of saying.

2.1.2 Their most powerful argument is this: in the scenario proposed, they say:

> This is false: Socrates says a falsehood,

---
[4] According to Dutilh Novaes, 'Form and Matter in Later Latin Medieval Logic', p. 343: "formally defective arguments would be those that do not display a valid [...] mood, while materially defective arguments are those with false premises." She traces the distinction to Aristotle's *Metaphysics* Δ (1013b19–20) and comments by Alexander of Aphrodisias, and finds it in medieval authors such as al-Ghazali and Kilwardby.
[5] Cassationists take their name from the Latin verb 'cassare', to nullify, to render useless or void (preserved in English as the verb 'to cass' in Scots law). See 'Introduction', §1.

sicut planum est, sed non potest esse falsa nisi ex altera istarum causarum: aut quia nihil dicit aut quia aliquid dicit sed illud est verum sed non ex secunda causa, ergo ex prima.

ad 2.1.1 Sed ista positio negat sensum. Talis enim sic dicens:

    Ego dico falsum,

fatigatur ex loquela, si diu sic dicat, similiter aliquos audientes gravat in casu, quod non esset si ipse nihil diceret cum alii non audiant nisi quod ipse loquitur.

Similiter videns istam propositionem:

    Ego nihil video,

aliquid videt.

ad 2.1 Constat similiter quantum ad hoc quod ponunt omne insolubile ortum habere ex actu nostro expresso in insolubili ⟨quod⟩ hoc est falsum. In hoc enim:

    Falsum est,

nullus actus noster exprimitur, posito tamen quod ista sola sit. Quod accidit in aliis insolubilibus.

ad 2.1.2 Ad rationem istius positionis patet quod non concludit; hec enim falsa est:

    Falsum dicitur a Sorte,

sed non ex aliqua illarum duarum causarum, sed quia denotat falsum dici a Sorte, quod non dicitur ab eo, sicut plenius determinabitur in processu.

⟨Solventes secundum peccatum in materia: Solutio Thomae Bradwardyn⟩

2.2 Alii respondentes ad huiusmodi paralogismos nullum assignant defectum in paralogismo, sed in uno alio paralogismo ponunt defectum in materia, negantes alteram premissarum, unde dicente Sorte istam:

    Sortes dicit falsum,

que sit A, dicunt quod A est | falsum. Et cum arguitur:

    A est falsum et A dicitur a Sorte, ergo falsum dicitur
    a Sorte,

E_8 22va

---

2 sed^1] et E_4 3 secunda causa] quarta E_4 7 ipse] *om.* E_4 16 nullus] est falsus unus E_4 || sit] aliter scit *add.* E_8 16–17 Quod accidit *corr.*] *inv.* mss 18 quod] hoc *add.* E_4 || hec] est *add.* E_4 22 non] omnino E_8 25–26 assignant defectum] *inv.* E_4 27 istam] ista E_4 29 est] sit E_4

as is evident. But it can only be false because of one of two reasons: either because he says nothing or because he says something that is true, but not for the second reason, hence because of the first.

ad 2.1.1 But this solution denies the evidence of our senses. For if someone saying this:

> I say a falsehood

says it for a long time he ⟨will be⟩ worn out from speaking, ⟨and⟩ similarly ⟨will⟩ wear down some of his listeners in the scenario, but that could hardly be the case if he said nothing, given that others hear only what he says.

Similarly, someone seeing this proposition:

> I see nothing

sees something.

ad 2.1 Concerning their claim that every insoluble has its origin from an act of ours expressed in the insoluble, it is similarly certain that it is false. For in this:

> A falsehood exists

no act of ours is expressed, supposing, however, that this is the only proposition. The same happens in other insolubles.

ad 2.1.2 Regarding the grounds for this solution: it is clear that they are not persuasive; for this is false:

> A falsehood is said by Socrates,

but it is not because of either of those two reasons,[6] but because it means that a falsehood is said by Socrates which is not said by him, as will be explained more fully in what follows.[7]

⟨Solutions according to errors in matter: Bradwardine's solution⟩

2.2 Others responding to these sorts of paralogisms find no defect in the ⟨initial⟩ paralogism, but in a further paralogism they claim there is a defect in matter,[8] denying one of the premises. Thus supposing Socrates says this:

> Socrates says a falsehood,

call it A, they say that A is false. And when one argues:

> A is a falsehood, and A is said by Socrates, so a falsehood is said by Socrates,

---

[6] See §2.1.2: "because he says nothing or because he says something true".
[7] See §3.4.
[8] That is, in its premises.

concedunt consequentiam et antecedens et consequens similiter, et ita nullum defectum assignant, cum tamen ille sit paralogismus, ut patebit in processu. Et cum arguitur ultra:

Hec est vera 'Sortes dicit falsum' et Sortes dicit hanc et solum hanc, ergo dicit verum,

negant minorem: illam enim quam ego propono non dicit Sortes, sed sibi similem.

2.2.1 Ratio autem istius positionis est hec: dicit hec [pro]positio quod pars potest supponere pro suo toto, et hoc indifferenter respectu cuiuscumque predicati et respectu cuiuscumque copule, unde A, quam dicit Sortes, significat se falsam dici a Sorte, et ita significat se esse falsam et veram similiter, quia quelibet propositio significans se non esse veram significat se esse veram, ut dicit positio. Et ita illa quam dicit Sortes, est falsa pro se ipsa, sed illa quam ego dico ⟨et⟩ similis est ei secundum vocem, vera est. Illa enim quam ego dico verificatur pro consimili dicta a Sorte, sed illam quam ego dico non dicit Sortes, ut si dicat Sortes:

Sortes dicit falsum,

que sit A, dicunt quod A significat se esse falsam et veram similiter, sed ⟨si⟩ ego propono:

Sortes dicit falsum,

que sit B, dicunt quod B est simpliciter vera pro A dicta a Sorte.

2.2.2 Contra istam positionem arguitur multipliciter. Primo sic: A quam dicit Sortes est falsa, ergo eius contradictoria erit vera:

Nullum falsum dicitur a Sorte,

et tu concedes quod falsum dicitur a Sorte, ergo erunt ista simul vera:

Falsum dicitur a Sorte

et:

Nullum falsum dicitur a Sorte,

que apparent contradictorie.

2.2.3 Contra hoc arguitur aliter sic: proponatur hec vel scribatur:

---

1 concedunt consequentiam] conceditur consequentia E_8 || ita] ista E_4 2–3 cum ... processu] *om.* E_8 6 enim] *om.* E_4 || ego propono] expono E_4 8 dicit] quod *add.* E_8 12 similiter] simpliciter E_4 13 veram] *om.* E_4 || positio] *om.* E_4 14 similis est] *inv.* E_4 15 illam *corr.*] aliam *a.c.* idem *p.c.* E_4 illa E_8 16 si] quia E_4 21 est simpliciter] *inv.* E_4 23 est] esse E_4 || erit vera] sed E_4 25 ergo erunt] *inv.* E_4 29 que apparent contradictorie] que apparet contradicere E_8 quia apparent contradictorie E_4 30 arguitur aliter] arguo E_8 || proponatur] ponatur E_4

they grant the inference and the premises and the conclusion similarly, and thus assign no defect—although in fact it is a paralogism, as will be clear in what follows. And when one argues further:

> 'Socrates says a falsehood' is true and Socrates says this and only this, so he says a truth,

they deny the minor premise, for Socrates does not say the proposition I assert, but a proposition similar to it.[9]

2.2.1 Now the ground for this solution is this: this solution says that the part can supposit for its whole and this indifferently for any predicate and any copula.[10] Hence A, which Socrates says, signifies itself to be a false utterance of Socrates', and thus signifies itself to be false—and also to be true because any proposition signifying itself not to be true signifies itself to be true, so the solution claims.[11] And thus the proposition uttered by Socrates is false about itself, but the one which I utter, which is similar to it syntactically, is true. For the proposition which I utter is true about the similar utterance of Socrates', but Socrates does not utter the proposition which I utter; e.g., if Socrates says:

> Socrates says a falsehood,

call it A, they say that A signifies itself to be false and also true, but ⟨if⟩ I claim

> Socrates says a falsehood,

call it B, they say that B is unconditionally true about A, which is uttered by Socrates.[12]

2.2.2 I argue against this solution in many ways, first like this: A, which Socrates says, is false, so its contradictory will be true:

> No falsehood is said by Socrates,

and you grant that a falsehood is said by Socrates, so these will be true together:

> A falsehood is said by Socrates,

and

> No falsehood is said by Socrates,

which appear to be contradictories.

2.2.3 I argue in another way against this argument like this: let this proposition be proposed or written:

---

[9] See Bradwardine, *Insolubilia*, §ad 7.1.1.
[10] This is Bradwardine's third postulate: *Insolubilia*, §6.3.
[11] This is Bradwardine's second conclusion: *Insolubilia*, §6.4.
[12] An allusion to Bradwardine's appeal to the fallacy *secundum quid et simpliciter* to characterize his solution to the insolubles: see Bradwardine, *Insolubilia*, §ad 7.11.

Hoc est falsum,

que sit A et demonstrato per aliam, li B, hoc toto A, quod est possibile secundum hanc positionem, tunc A est falsum. Concedatur; ergo eius contradictorium est | verum:

E_8 22vb

Hoc non est falsum,

vel:

Nihil quod est ⟨hoc est⟩ falsum,

et tu concede⟨s⟩ quod A est falsum, ergo eodem precise demonstrato ista erunt simul vera:

Hoc est falsum,

et:

Nihil quod est hoc est falsum,

quod non capit mens.

2.2.3.1 Preterea: ex opposito ipsius A arguitur sic:

Nihil quod est hoc est falsum, A est hoc, | ergo A non est falsum.

E_4 159rb

Maior est vera et minor, et tamen negatur conclusio secundum istam [pro]positionem et ideo dicitur negando consequentiam.

Sed contra: maior est universalis negativa denotans predicatum negari a quolibet demonstrato in subiecto, et in minori accipitur subiectum unum pro quo supponit subiectum ⟨maioris⟩, ergo iste sillogismus regitur per dici de nullo. Sic ergo dicendo negatur evidentissimum fundamentum sillogismorum.

Sed dicitur quod etsi subiectum supponat pro A in maiori non tamen denotatur predicatum removeri ab illo.

Contra: cum maior sit universalis negativa denotabit predicatum removeri ab aliquo demonstrato per subiectum, et nihil demonstratur ibi nisi A, per casum, ergo in maiori denotatur predicatum removeri ab A.

2.2.3.2 Preterea: secundum istam positionem sequitur quod aliqua universalis est vera cuius aliqua singularis est falsa, ymmo cuius multe singulares sunt false, et similiter indefinita falsa cuius autem aliqua singularis est vera, quia [subiectum] oppositum ipsius A est verum et tamen singularis

---

2 demonstrato] eodem preter se *scr. sed del.* E_8 || aliam] alium E_8 *om.* E_4 || toto *corr.*] totum *mss* 3 Concedatur] conceditur E_4 8 precise] preciso E_4 12 est hoc] *om.* E_4 14 A] *om.* E_4 24 etsi] si E_4 || non tamen] *om.* E_8 27 A] *om.* E_4 30 cuius^2] cum E_4 31 indefinita] infinita E_4 || cuius] cum E_8 32 oppositum] *om.* E_4

This is a falsehood,

call it A, where the whole of A is referred to by ⟨the subject of⟩ another ⟨instance of 'This is a falsehood'⟩, call it B, which is possible according to this solution.¹³ Then A is false ⟨and B is true⟩. If this is granted, then ⟨A⟩'s contradictory is true:

This is not a falsehood

or

Nothing which is this is a falsehood;

and you grant that A is false, so these will be true together:

This is a falsehood

and

Nothing which is this is a falsehood,

referring precisely to the same thing ⟨*viz* A⟩, which is incomprehensible.

2.2.3.1 Moreover: I argue from the opposite of A like this:

Nothing which is this is a falsehood, A is this, so A is not a falsehood.

The major premise is true as well as the minor, and yet the conclusion is denied according to this solution, and so the validity of the inference must be denied.

On the contrary: the major is a universal negative meaning that the predicate is denied of anything referred to by the subject, and in the minor one object is taken for which the subject ⟨of the major⟩ supposits, so this syllogism is governed by the rule "dici de nullo", so by saying ⟨that the validity of the inference must be denied⟩ the most evident ground of syllogisms is denied.¹⁴

But it is said ⟨in reply⟩ that even if the subject supposits for A in the major, the meaning, however, is that the predicate is not separated from it.

On the contrary: since the major is a universal negative it will mean that the predicate is separated from anything referred to by the subject, and nothing is referred to in the major except A, by hypothesis, so in the major the meaning is that the predicate is separated from A.

2.2.3.2 Moreover: according to this solution, it follows that some universal proposition is true one of whose singulars¹⁵ is false, indeed, many of its singulars are false—and similarly, that an indefinite is false some singular of which is true—because the opposite of A is a true ⟨universal⟩ but the

---

¹³ As set out in §2.2.1 above.
¹⁴ It's a syllogism in Celarent, which is directly supported by the "dici de nullo" ("to be said of none"): see Aristotle, *Prior Analytics*, I 1, 24b30–31.
¹⁵ This is the syntactic singular as defined in §1 above.

ubi demonstratur A est falsa. Et secundum positionem istam conceditur totum istud quia ista:

    Nihil quod est A est falsum

habet istas duas singulares:

    A non est falsum,

et:

    A est verum,

et illas significat disiunctive, particularis autem opposita illas significat copulative. Sed istud videtur mirabile. Magis enim deberet esse modo contrario secundum | processum Aristotelis. 'Omne' enim et talia signa universalia non significant universale sed quoniam universaliter secundum Aristotelem in libro Peryarmenias, et hoc est facere terminum communem sibi adiunctum copulative supponere pro quolibet sui ⟨inferiori⟩ secundum omnes exponentes.   E₈ 23ra

2.2.3.3 Preterea: hoc quod dicitur quod ista:

    A est verum,

est singularis huius universalis, quod est:

    ⟨Nihil quod est⟩ A est falsum,

est manifeste falsum quia hec universalis est mere negativa, sicut patet, ergo nihil ponit affirmando sicut nec ista:

    Cesar non est,

que nihil ponit esse; tamen quia predicatum illius universalis est iste terminus 'falsum', respectu cuius accipiende sunt singulares propositiones, hec autem singularis:

    A est verum

non convenit cum illa universali in predicato, ymmo et simile esset dicere quod

    Sortes est niger

est singularis huius:

    Nihil quod est Sortes est album,

quod est manifeste falsum.

---

1 positionem istam] *inv.* E₄   2 istud] quod *add.* E₈   8 illas significat²] *inv.* E₄   17 est singularis] *inv.* E₄   22 que] et E₈   30 album] albus E₄

singular proposition where A is referred to is false; and according to this solution the whole is granted, because this:

> Nothing which is A is a falsehood,

has these two singulars:

> A is not a falsehood

and

> A is a truth,[16]

and it signifies them disjunctively, while the particular proposition which is the opposite ⟨of the universal⟩ signifies them conjunctively. But that seems miraculous, for it should rather be in the other way round according to Aristotle's thought. For 'every' and such universal quantifiers do not signify a universal but instead signify universally according to Aristotle in the *Perihermeneias*,[17] and ⟨to signify universally⟩ is to make a general term adjoined to it supposit conjunctively for any of its ⟨inferiors⟩ by means of all the exponents.

2.2.3.3 Moreover: to say that this:

> A is a truth

is a singular of the universal proposition, namely

> ⟨Nothing which is⟩ A is a falsehood,

is manifestly false because this universal proposition is purely negative, as is clear; hence it claims nothing affirmatively, just as neither does this:

> Caesar does not exist,

which does not claim anything to exist. However, because the predicate of that universal proposition[18] is the term 'falsehood', in respect of which the singular propositions should be taken—whereas this singular:

> A is a truth,

does not agree with the universal in the predicate—it would be like saying that

> Socrates is black

is a singular of

> Nothing which is Socrates is white,

which is manifestly false.

---

[16] According to Bradwardine, A (that is, 'This is a falsehood') signifies conjunctively that A is a falsehood and A is true. So its opposite (that is, 'Nothing which is this is a falsehood') is a universal negative proposition which signifies disjunctively that A is not a falsehood or that A is not true. These conjuncts and disjuncts, which are parts of what A and its opposite signify, are also described by Bradwardine as singulars of A and its opposite: see Bradwardine, *Insolubilia*, §ad 7.6.

[17] See Aristotle, *De Interpretatione*, ch. 7, 17b11–12 (tr. Boethius, ed. Minio-Paluello, p. 10, 14–15); Hamesse, *Les Auctoritates Aristotelis*, p. 305 #11.

[18] That is, 'Nothing which is A is a falsehood'.

Et ideo dicitur quod hec est singularis subiecti etsi non propositionis.

Sed contra: subiectum istius universalis est terminus singularis non habens nisi unum suppositum, puta A, ergo etc.

2.2.4 Preterea: ista [pro]positio ponit[ur] quod una talis:

>   Falsum dicitur a Sorte

est vera pro una simili falsa. Pono ergo quod iste due simul sint:

>   Falsum est

et:

>   Falsum est,

et nulla alia, et sit una A et alia B. Quero tunc an A sit verum vel falsum. Si verum, ergo eadem ratione B est verum, cum non sit maior ratio de una quam de alia, ergo nihil est falsum, ergo propositio ⟨A⟩ dicens falsum esse est falsa. Si A est falsum, ergo B est verum quia hec positio ponit quod una talis potest verificari pro consimili falsa. Consequens tamen est falsum cum non sit maior ratio quare una debeat esse vera quam alia.

Ideo dicitur negando consequentiam:

>   A est falsum, ergo B est verum,

quia utraque illarum significat se esse veram et falsam.

Sed contra: ergo ita foret in aliis quia de similibus simile est iudicium, ergo si una talis foret falsa:

>   Sortes dicit falsum,

quelibet consimilis foret falsa. Similiter ista:

>   Falsum est

secundum istam positionem non significat se esse falsam nisi nullo alio existente falso, ergo posito quod A falsum sit, B non significat se esse falsum.

Si dicatur quod A significat se esse falsum etiam alio falso existente, contra: cum non sit maior ratio quare significet se esse falsum uno falso existente quam alio, sequitur quod semper significaret se esse falsum. Consequens falsum quia aliquando est vera.

---

2 istius] huius E_4 3 puta] *om.* E_4 8–9 et ... est] *om.* E_8 13 est³] *om.* E_4 15 maior] falsa *add.* E_4 17 B] una E_4 22 foret] esset (*dub.*) E_4 27 A] minor *a.c.* B *p.c.* E_4 ‖ etiam] et E_8 28 significet] significaret E_4 30 est vera] *inv.* E_4

And so it ⟨might be⟩ said that it is a singular of the subject even if not of the proposition.

But on the contrary: the subject of this universal is a singular term having only one supposit, namely A, hence ⟨that A is the singular of the universal proposition is manifestly false⟩.

2.2.4 Moreover: this solution claims that one proposition like this:

> A falsehood is said by Socrates

is true about a falsehood similar to it. Hence suppose that there are these two together:

> A falsehood exists

and

> A falsehood exists

and no others, let one be A and the other B. Then I ask whether A is true or false. If ⟨A is⟩ true, then for the same reason B is true, since there is no more reason why one rather than the other. So nothing is false, so the proposition, ⟨that is, A,⟩ saying that a falsehood exists is false. If A is false, then B is true because this solution claims that one of them can be true about a falsehood similar ⟨to it⟩. But the conclusion is false since there is no more reason why one should be true than the other.

So one reply is to deny the inference:

> A is false, therefore B is true,

because each of them signifies itself to be true and false.

But on the contrary: then it would be like that in other cases because there should be a similar judgment about similar things, therefore if one proposition like this was false:

> Socrates says a falsehood,

any proposition similar to it would be false. Similarly, this:

> A falsehood exists,

only signifies itself to be false according to this solution if there is no other falsehood, so supposing that A is false, B does not signify itself to be false.

If it is said that A signifies itself to be false even when there is another falsehood, on the contrary: since there is no more reason why it should signify itself to be false when one falsehood exists rather than another, it follows that ⟨A⟩ would always signify itself to be false. The conclusion is false because sometimes ⟨A⟩ is true.

2.2.5 Preterea: supponatur quod Sortes et Petrus sint simul in eadem domo et dicat Sortes:

Falsum est in domo,

que sit A, et dicat Petrus simul:

Falsum est in domo,

que sit B. Queritur tunc utrum A sit verum vel falsum. Si verum, ergo B est verum eadem ratione, et ultra: ergo nullum falsum est in domo, posito quod tantum iste due propositiones sint. Ideo dicitur quod utraque est falsa.

Sed contra: si Sortes diceret istam propositionem extra domum:

Falsum est in domo,

tunc illa foret vera pro B dicta a Petro in domo secundum istam positionem. Sed manifestum est quod idem significat omnino et eodem modo ista propositio prolata extra domum et intra. Sed extra domum prolata verificatur pro B, ergo in domo similiter.

Et istud confirmatur per hoc quod propositio non mutatur de veritate in falsitatem nisi per mutationem factam ex parte rei, sed tota res pro qua verificatur extra domum manet non mutata ipsa existente in domo, ergo si pro hac re verificatur extra domum, pro eadem verificabitur in domo. In eo enim quod res est vel non est, oratio vera vel falsa est.[1] | E_8 23va

2.2.5.1 Preterea: significatum complexi consurgit ex significatis incomplexorum copulatis ad invicem, sicut patet ex processu in tertio De anima et libro Peryarmenias. Sed manifestum est quod termini incomplexi istius propositionis:

Falsum est in domo

idem significant in domo et extra domum, et eodem modo quantum in eis est, et eodem modo copulantur ad invicem in domo et extra domum, ergo significatum quod consurgit ex istis sic copulatis erit idem in domo et extra domum, cuius tamen oppositum ponit hec positio.

---

3 est in domo] esse in domo est in domo E_4 7 B] minor *a.c.* E_4 || ergo] *om.* E_8 8 due] *om.* E_4 9 est] sit E_4 10 si] *om.* E_4 12 pro] quod E_8 || Petro] dicta *add.* E_4 14 ista] *om.* E_4 18 manet] videt E_4 19 verificabitur] verificatur E_4 20 est[1]] *om.* E_4 || oratio ... est] est oratio vera vel falsa E_4 22 ex] in E_8 23 est] *om.* E_4 26 in domo] *om.* E_4 27 est] *om.* E_4 28 ergo] totum *add.* E_4

2.2.5 Moreover: suppose that Socrates and Peter are together in the same house and Socrates says:

> A falsehood exists inside the house,

call it A, and Peter says at the same time:

> A falsehood exists inside the house,

call it B. Then I ask whether A is true or false. If it is true, then B is true for the same reason; and moreover, therefore no falsehood exists inside the house, supposing that there are only these two propositions. Hence it is said that both are false.

But on the contrary: if Socrates were to say this proposition outside the house:

> A falsehood exists inside the house,

then it would be true about proposition B spoken by Peter inside the house, according to this solution. But it is evident that this proposition signifies altogether the same and in the same way uttered outside the house and inside. But uttered outside the house it is true about B, so inside the house too.

And this is confirmed by the fact that a proposition does not change from truth to falsehood except through a change made in reality, but everything about which it is true when outside the house remains unchanged when it is inside the house. Therefore if it is true about that thing when outside the house, it will be true about the same thing when inside the house. For an utterance is true or false insofar as things are or are not the case.

2.2.5.1 Moreover: the significate of a ⟨propositional⟩ complex derives from the mutual conjoining of the significates of the simple expressions, as is clear from the reasoning in the third book of the *De Anima* and from the *Perihermeneias*.[19] But it is evident that the simple terms of this proposition:

> A falsehood exists inside the house

signify the same thing inside the house and outside the house and signify in the same way in themselves and are mutually conjoined in the same way inside the house and outside the house. Therefore the significate which derives from those significates conjoined in this way will be the same inside the house and outside the house. But this solution claims the opposite.

---

[19] *On the Soul* III ch. 6 (430a26 ff.) and *De Interpretatione*, chs. 4–5.

2.2.6 Preterea: posito quod Sortes dicat:

> Falsum dicitur a vidente,

et Plato sic dicat:

> Nullum falsum dicitur a vidente,

posito quod uterque habeat oculos apertos, uterque contradiceret alteri secundum istam positionem, sed posito quod Plato clauderet oculos et diceret illud idem, non contradiceret Sorti. Sequitur ergo ex ista positione quod contradictio tollitur inter propositiones per motum palpebre, quod tamen est omnino irrationale.

2.2.7 Preterea: ista propositio:

> Falsum dicitur a Sorte,

non plus significat se dici a Sorte quam aliam quia supposito quod subiectum supponat pro tota ⟨propositione⟩ adhuc non plus supponit pro ista quam pro alia, sicut posito quod tantum Sortes curreret non plus significat ista propositio:

> Homo currit

Sorte currente quam Platone currente; subiectum enim equaliter significat Sortem et Platonem. Ex modo etiam supponendi non habet quod plus supponat pro uno quam pro alio quia supponit pro suis suppositis disiunctive, sed disiunctiva non plus significat unam suam partem esse veram quam aliam.

2.2.8 Preterea: significare est actio significantis, sed hec propositio:

> Falsum est

quantum est ex parte | sua eodem modo agit nullo alio falso existente et alio falso existente, quia non est agens cognoscens, sed nullo alio falso existente significat se esse falsam et hoc secundum sic dicentes, ergo alio | falso existente significabit se esse falsam et hoc passo eodem modo disposito, ut posito quod etsi aliud falsum sit, lateat tamen illud cum proponitur ista:

---

3 dicat *corr.*] dicit *mss et add.* E₄   5 habeat] haberet E₄   ‖ apertos] vides E₄   8 tollitur inter propositiones] inter propositiones tollitur E₄   9 est omnino] *inv.* E₄   17 equaliter] equale E₈   18 supponendi] supponendo E₈   ‖ quod] *om.* E₈   20 suam] *om.* E₈   22 hec] *om.* E₈   24 sua] sui E₄   26 falsam *corr.*] falsum *mss*   26–27 secundum sic ... et hoc] *add. supra lineam* E₄   28 illud] illum E₈   29 proponitur] proponi E₄

2.2.6 Moreover: supposing that Socrates says:

> A falsehood is said by one seeing,

and Plato says this:

> No falsehood is said by one seeing,

supposing that both have their eyes open, each would contradict the other according to this solution. But supposing that Plato closed his eyes and said the same thing, he would not contradict Socrates. Therefore, it follows from this solution that a contradiction between propositions is removed through the movement of the eyelid, which, however, is completely unreasonable.[20]

2.2.7 Moreover: this proposition:

> A falsehood is said by Socrates,

no more signifies itself to be said by Socrates than it does any other proposition. For, supposing that the subject supposits for the whole proposition, still, it no more supposits for this proposition than for another; just as supposing that only Socrates were running, this proposition:

> A man is running,

no more signifies ⟨that Socrates is running⟩ when Socrates is running than ⟨it signifies that Plato is running⟩ when Plato is running. For the subject equally signifies Socrates and Plato. Also from the mode of supposition[21] it does not supposit more for one than for the other, because it supposits for its supposita disjunctively, but a disjunctive proposition no more signifies one of its disjuncts to be true than another.

2.2.8 Moreover: to signify is an act of the one who signifies, but this proposition:

> A falsehood exists,

in itself acts in the same way whether no other falsehood exists or another falsehood exists, because it does not have a mind of its own. But if no other falsehood exists it signifies itself to be false, at least according to those advocating this solution. Therefore even if another falsehood exists it will still signify itself to be false, and this while the words are arranged in the same way. E.g., supposing that even if another falsehood exists, yet let it be hidden when this is proposed:

---

[20] Segrave appears here to adapt Burley's notorious refutation of Ockham's account of the signification of terms, which seems to imply that it could be affected merely by the movement of a finger: see, e.g., Read, 'Logic in the Latin West in the Fourteenth Century', pp. 147–48.

[21] On modes of supposition, see, e.g., Read, 'Medieval Theories of Properties of Terms', §3. In 'A man is running', 'man' has determinate supposition, which is explained by Ockham and others in terms of descent to and ascent from a disjunction of singulars of the original proposition.

> Falsum est,

et ita posito alio falso, foret hec falsa:

> Falsum est;

consequens est falsum, et ita patet falsitas illius dicti voluntarii et absque ratione.

Capitulum Tertium
⟨Solventes secundum peccatum in forma⟩

3.0 Preter positiones iam dictas sunt alie ponentes insolubilia peccantia in forma, et illi sunt bipartiti. Quidam solvunt illa secundum quid et simpliciter, et quidam secundum fallaciam accidentis.

⟨Solventes secundum fallaciam secundum quid et simpliciter⟩

3.1 Solventes secundum quid et simpliciter negant consequentiam:

> Hoc falsum dicitur a Sorte, ergo falsum dicitur a Sorte.

Dicunt quod pars in talibus ubi accidit reflexio eiusdem supra se cum verbo pertinente ad motus anime non supponit pro toto, et ideo dicens hoc falsum non dicit falsum simpliciter sed secundum quid. Isti etiam sic dicentes diversimode dicunt.

3.2 Quidam dicunt quod dicens se dicere falsum nihil dicit, nec aliquale dicit nec propositionem dicit; sed dicit hoc aliquid, et hoc est dicere aliquid secundum quid et ⟨non⟩ simpliciter, hoc aliquale et non simpliciter aliquale. Sed constat quod isti errant. Talis enim sic dicens loquitur, ergo aliquid loquitur. Similiter sic dicens dicit litteras et sillabas, ergo aliquid dicit et aliquale. Similiter videns istam:

---

2 alio falso] alia falsa E_4 6 Capitulum Tertium] *in marg.* E_8 8 positiones] ponentes E_4 || dictas *corr.*] dictis E_8 dicto E_4 || alie] alii E_4 || peccantia] peccante E_4 9 Quidam] enim *add.* E_4 15 reflexio] inflexio E_4 23 loquitur] *om.* E_4

A falsehood exists,

and so supposing there is another falsehood, this:

A falsehood exists,

will ⟨still⟩ be false.[22] The conclusion is false, and thus the falsity is clear of that claim ⟨that 'A falsehood exists' signifies itself to be false⟩, one which is arbitrary and without reason.

Chapter 3
⟨Solutions according to defects in form⟩

3.0 Besides the solutions already described there are others claiming that insolubles are defective in form, and they are of two kinds. Some people solve them by the fallacy of the conditional and the unconditional, and some by the fallacy of accident.

⟨Solutions according to the fallacy of the conditional and the unconditional⟩[23]

3.1 Those who solve ⟨insolubles⟩ by the fallacy of the conditional and the unconditional deny the inference:

This falsehood is said by Socrates, so a falsehood is said by Socrates.

They claim that in such propositions where reflection occurs of a part on itself with a verb pertaining to intentional acts, that part does not supposit for the whole, and so anyone saying this falsehood does not say a falsehood unconditionally but conditionally. There are also different ways in which those advocating this solution sustain it.

3.2 Some claim that anyone saying that he says a falsehood says nothing, that he neither says anything true or false nor says a proposition;[24] but he says a this-something,[25] and this is to say something conditionally and not unconditionally, a this-something true or false and not just anything true or false unconditionally. But it is certain that they are wrong. For anyone speaking like this is speaking, so saying something ⟨unconditionally⟩. Similarly, anyone speaking like this is uttering letters and syllables,

---

[22] By Bradwardine's second conclusion. See n. 11 above.
[23] On the fallacy *secundum quid et simpliciter* (that is, of the conditional and the unconditional), see, e.g., Bradwardine, *Insolubilia*, 'Introduction', 5–6.
[24] We have followed Nuchelmans, 'The Distinction *actus exercitus/actus significatus* in Medieval Semantics', p. 76 in translating 'aliquale' (literally, 'of some kind') as 'true or false', since those are the kinds that are relevant here.
[25] 'A this-something' is the standard English translation of a classic Aristotelian term of art, 'tode ti', rendered into Latin as 'hoc aliquid', referring to the primary substance. For discussion, see, e.g., Cohen and Reeve, 'Aristotle's Metaphysics', §6.

Falsum videtur a me,

scriptam in litteris aureis, videt aurum, ergo aliquid videt. Sic igitur dicentes negant sensum.

3.3 Sed alii concedunt quod sic videns aliquid videt simpliciter et aliquale simpliciter, et negant consequentiam: ergo verum simpliciter vel falsum simpliciter, et [tamen] ⟨ratio⟩ est quia pro aliquo supposito huius termini 'verum' vel huius termini 'falsum' potest iste terminus 'aliquid' supponere simpliciter pro quo non potest iste terminus 'verum' vel 'falsum'. Non enim, ut dicunt, si dicere hoc falsum sit | dicere aliquid simpliciter, propter hoc dicere hoc falsum est dicere falsum simpliciter.

3.3.1 Et ratio istorum est quia Aristoteles secundo Elencorum videtur solvere huiusmodi paralogismos quales dicuntur insolubiles secundum quid et simpliciter, ut iurans se esse periurum aut est periurus aut non. Similiter dicens se mentiri aut mentitur aut non.

3.4 Sed isti, etsi probabilius dicant inter omnes, constat quod non recte solvunt quia recta solutio est manifestatio falsi sillogismi secundum quemlibet defectum ⟨secundum quem⟩ accidit falsum, ut patet secundo

---

2 videt²] *om.* E₄   9 si] sic E₈ *dub.* E₄   10 hoc²] est *add.* E₄   14 mentitur] mentitus E₈
15 probabilius] probabiliter E₄

so he says something and ⟨something true or false⟩. Similarly, anyone seeing this:

> A falsehood is seen by me,

written in gold letters sees gold, so he sees something ⟨unconditionally⟩. Therefore, those advocating this ⟨solution⟩ deny the evidence of the senses.[26]

3.3 But others grant that anyone seeing in this way sees something unconditionally and something true or false unconditionally, and they deny the inference: "therefore a truth unconditionally or a falsehood unconditionally". This is because the term 'something' can supposit unconditionally for some suppositum of the term 'truth' or the term 'falsehood' for which the term 'truth' or 'falsehood' cannot supposit. For, they claim, if saying this falsehood is saying something unconditionally it does not follow that saying this falsehood is saying a falsehood unconditionally.[27]

3.3.1 Their reason is because Aristotle in the second book of the *Sophistical Refutations* seems to solve paralogisms of the kind called insolubles by the fallacy of the conditional and the unconditional, e.g., anyone swearing that he is forsworn is either forsworn or not.[28] Similarly, anyone saying he is lying is either lying or not.[29]

3.4 But even if they have the most plausible claim of everyone, it is certain that they do not solve the insolubles correctly, because the correct solution is the exhibition of a false syllogism according to whatever defect yields falsehood, as is clear from the second book of the *Sophistical Refutations*.[30]

---

[26] Segrave's criticism here echoes and expands on Bradwardine's attack on the second group of cassationists (cassantes actum): see Bradwardine, *Insolubilia*, §5.6. They may be one of the groups of those appealing to the fallacy of the conditional and unconditional discussed by ps.-Sherwood (ed. Roure, 'La problématique des propositions insolubles', pp. 253–61): see Nuchelmans, 'The Distinction *actus exercitus/actus significatus*', p. 76 ff. See also the solutions offered by Scotus in his *Questions on the Sophisticis Elenchis*, Qq. 52–53 (*Opera Omnia*, ed. Vivès, vol. II, pp. 73–76): see also Nuchelmans, op. cit., pp. 78–80.

[27] This may be a reference to Richard Kilvington's solution. He wrote: "I say, then, that no insoluble that is presently under discussion is absolutely true or absolutely false; instead each is true in a certain respect and false in a certain respect" (Dico, igitur, quod nullum insolubile de quo praesens est locutio est simpliciter verum vel simpliciter falsum; sed quodlibet est verum secundum quid et falsum secundum quid). See B. and N. Kretzmann, *The Sophismata of Richard Kilvington*, p. 142. More generally, the restrictivist claim is that what the terms 'true' (or 'truth') and 'false' (or 'falsehood') can supposit for is restricted in a way that other terms, like 'something', are not restricted.

[28] Segrave explains what he means by 'being forsworn' ('periurare') in §3.6.1 below.

[29] *Sophistical Refutations*, ch. 25, 180a38–b7.

[30] See Aristotle, *De Sophisticis Elenchis*, tr. Boethius, 40: "Quoniam autem est recta quidem solutio manifestatio falsi sillogismi secundum quemlibet interrogationem accidit falsum." Cf. *Sophistical Refutations*, ch. 18, 176b29–30 (see also 176b31–a8 and ch. 24, 179b6–33, esp. 23–24).

Elencorum. Sed isti solventes secundum quid et simpliciter non manifestant quemlibet defectum. Peccant enim secundum accidens quia sic arguendo:

> Hoc dicitur a Sorte et hoc est falsum, ergo falsum dicitur a Sorte,

iste terminus 'falsum' pro aliquo supponit in minori pro quo non supponit in conclusione. Similiter sic arguendo:

> Nullum falsum dicitur a Sorte, hoc est falsum, ergo hoc non dicitur a Sorte,

variatur medium quia pro alio supponit iste terminus 'falsum' in maiori et minori, et hoc secundum sic dicentes. Et ita patet quod isti habent solvere huiusmodi paralogismos secundum fallaciam accidentis, scilicet ex variatione medii vel extremi.

3.5 Preterea: non videtur quod convenienter solvantur secundum quid et simpliciter quia in talibus non arguitur a quo ad simpliciter quia si sic, dicens hoc falsum diceret falsum secundum quid. Consequens est falsum quia si ista determinatio 'secundum quid' determinet li dicere, falsa est. Dicere enim hoc falsum est simpliciter dicere. Si determinet li falsum, falsa est, quia hoc falsum est falsum simpliciter. Similiter in omni paralogismo secundum quid et simpliciter accipitur aliquis terminus cum aliquo privative vel diminute ab | eodem accepto simpliciter, sicut ens ymaginabile et ens simpliciter. Sic hec conditio 'mortuum' privat significatum huius[modi] termini 'homo' et ita de omnibus paralogismis illius fallacie. Sed in proposito determinatio addita termino non est diminuens sed ponens quia respicit predicationem eiusdem accepti simpliciter. Omne enim quod est hoc falsum est falsum, quod non est in paralogismis illius fallacie. Non enim omne ymaginabile est ens nec omne album secundum dentes est album, et hoc magis patet in hoc exemplo:

> Hoc falsum est, ergo falsum est,

demonstrata in antecedente ista:

> Falsum est

---

2 Peccant] peccat E$_4$ 6 terminus falsum] *inv.* E$_4$ 10 quia] *om.* E$_4$ 10–11 in ... minori] in minori et in maiori E$_4$ 12 scilicet] et E$_4$ 15 non] *om.* E$_8$ || ad] et *add.* E$_4$ 16 falsum³] sed *add.* E$_4$ 18 falsum est] *inv.* E$_8$ 19 est falsum simpliciter] simpliciter est falsum E$_4$ 20 aliquo] contradictione *add.* E$_4$ 22 Sic] *om.* E$_8$ 24 est] *om.* E$_8$ 26 Non] est *add.* E$_4$

But those solving them by the fallacy of the conditional and the unconditional do not exhibit every defect. For it commits the fallacy of accident because by arguing like this:

> This is said by Socrates and this is a falsehood, so a falsehood is said by Socrates,

the term 'falsehood' supposits in the minor premise for something it does not supposit for in the conclusion. Similarly, in arguing like this:

> No falsehood is said by Socrates, this is a falsehood, so this is not said by Socrates,

there is a variation in the middle term because the term 'falsehood' supposits for one thing in the major premise and another in the minor, according to those advocating this solution. And thus it is clear that they have to solve these kinds of paralogisms according to the fallacy of accident, namely, from a variation of the middle term or of an extreme term.[31]

3.5 Moreover: it does not seem that such paralogisms are feasibly solved by the fallacy of the conditional and the unconditional because in such cases it is not argued from something conditional to something unconditional, for if so, anyone saying this falsehood would say a falsehood conditionally. The conclusion is false because if this delimitation 'conditionally' delimits 'say', it is false. For to say this falsehood is to say it unconditionally. If ⟨'conditionally'⟩ delimits 'falsehood', it is false, because this falsehood is a falsehood unconditionally. Similarly, in every paralogism of the conditional and unconditional some term is taken with another term taken privatively or diminishingly with respect to the same term taken unconditionally, e.g., imaginable thing and thing unconditionally.[32] In this way, the qualification 'dead' is privative of the significate of the term 'man' and thus in all paralogisms committing this fallacy, but in the present example the delimitation added to the term is not diminishing but positive because it refers to its predication of the same thing taken unconditionally. For everything which is this falsehood is a falsehood which is not ⟨so⟩ in the paralogisms of this fallacy. For not everything imaginable is a thing nor is everything with white teeth white. This is clearer in this example:

> This falsehood exists, so a falsehood exists,

where the premise does not refer to:

> A falsehood exists

---

[31] The identification of the fallacy of accident with a variation (in the supposition) of the middle term or one of the extremes in a syllogism was a popular explanation of this fallacy in the thirteenth century, but was strongly rejected by Ockham. See, e.g., Gelber, 'The Fallacy of Accident and the "dictum de omni"', esp. §II.

[32] Segrave gives examples both of terms taken privatively, as when we speak of a dead man, who is not a man at all, and of terms taken diminishingly (diminutive), as when we speak of an imaginable thing, which is nonetheless a thing.

non simpliciter. Et ita patet quod quelibet conditio ibi posita est ponens et non diminuens. Non sunt igitur solvendi huiusmodi paralogismi secundum quid et simpliciter, reverentia tamen sic dicentium salva.

ad 3.3.1 Ad rationem istius positionis que videtur probabilis quia Aristoteles videtur tales sillogismos solvere secundum hanc fallaciam, dico quod nullus paralogismus quem Aristoteles ponit in capitulo de fallacia secundum quid et simpliciter est insolubilis, sicut nunc loquimur de insolubili.

3.6 Insolubile enim de quo modo loquimur servat dispositionem modi et figure secundum vocem, antecedente existente vero, conclusione tamen falsa, vel saltem reducibile est ad talem. Pro quo sciendum quod Aristoteles ponit ibi tres paralogismos qui videntur insolubiles et non sunt. Ut pateat veritas, formo illos:

3.6.1 Ponatur quod Sortes sic dicat iurando per dictum:

  Ego sum periurus.

Querit Aristoteles an bene iurat aut male. Si bene ergo verum est quod iurat, ergo est periurus quia hoc iurat. Si periurat, ergo verum est | quod iurat, ergo bene iurat, ergo non periurat. Et licet iste videatur insolubilis, tamen non est. E_8 24va

Pro quo sciendum est quod periurare est male iurare; male autem iurat non solum qui iurat falsum, sed et ille qui iurat verum cuius veritas dependet ex actu suo iurandi et cum hoc idem negatur ponit ipsum male facere. Unde constat quod sic iurans temere iurat. Veritas enim iuramenti debet dependere ex veritate iurati et non iuratum ex iuramento.

Dico ergo quod sic iurans periurat simpliciter. Ergo iurat verum. Concedo. Et cum | arguitur: Ergo bene iurat, nego consequentiam quia iurare verum non est simpliciter bene iurare, sed secundum quid, sicut albus secundum dentem non est albus simpliciter, sed requiritur plus, sicut dictum est, quod sit verum et quod non contrahat veritatem ex illo actu suo, et maxime si sit tale verum quod ponat ipsum male facere; bene tamen iurat secundum hoc quod est iurare verum, et hoc est quo et non simpliciter. E_4 159vb

---

1 conditio] conditionalis *a.c.* E_8 2 huiusmodi] isti E_4 7–8 de insolubili] *om.* E_4 9 modo] *om.* E_4 || loquimur] loquitur *in marg.* E_8 10 conclusione tamen] *inv.* E_4 11 reducibile *corr.*] reducibilis mss   14 dicat] Primus paralogismus *add. in marg.* E_8 16 an] quod E_4 17–18 ergo ... iurat] *add. in marg.* E_4 19 tamen] *om.* E_8 20 est[1]] *om.* E_4 22 idem *coniecimus*] illud mss   23 sic iurans] *inv.* E_4 26 verum] *om.* E_8 29 sit] sic E_4 30 verum] et *add.* E_8 || tamen] et non E_4 31 quo] quomodo (*dub.*) E_8

unconditionally. And thus it is clear that any condition placed there is positive and not diminishing. Therefore paralogisms of this kind are not to be solved by the fallacy of the conditional and the unconditional, with due respect to those who claim it is.

ad 3.3.1 Against the ground adduced by this solution, which seems plausible because Aristotle seems to solve such syllogisms by this fallacy, I say that no paralogism which Aristotle considers in the chapter ⟨of the *Sophistical Refutations*⟩ on the fallacy of the conditional and the unconditional is an insoluble as we are now speaking of an insoluble.

3.6 For an insoluble of which we are speaking observes the syntactic arrangement of mood and figure, where the premises are true but the conclusion false, or at least is reducible to that. In this regard, it should be noted that Aristotle there presents three paralogisms which seem to be insoluble but are not.[33] To make the truth plain, I form them:

3.6.1 Suppose that Socrates says this in swearing through ⟨his own⟩ proposition:

> I am forsworn.

Aristotle asks whether he swears well or badly.[34] If well, then what he swears is true, so he is forsworn because this is what he swears. If he is forsworn, then what he swears is true, so he swears well, so he is not forsworn. And although this ⟨paralogism⟩ seems to be insoluble, it is not, in fact.

Here it should be noted that to be forsworn is to swear badly; but someone who swears badly is not only one who swears a falsehood, but also one who swears a truth whose truth depends on his act of swearing and when that very thing is denied he claims that he acts badly. Hence it is certain that anyone swearing in this way swears rashly.[35] For the truth of an oath should depend on the truth of what is sworn, not what is sworn ⟨depend⟩ on the oath.

Therefore, I say that someone swearing in this way is unconditionally forsworn. So I grant that he swears the truth; and when one infers: "so he swears well", I deny the inference, because to swear the truth is not unconditionally to swear well, but conditionally, just as 'having white teeth' is not being white unconditionally. For it requires more, as was said, both that it is true and that it does not derive ⟨its⟩ truth from that act of his—and most particularly if it is the very truth that he claims that he acts badly. However, he does swear well insofar as he swears a truth—conditionally and not unconditionally.

---

[33] Aristotle, *Sophistical Refutations*, ch. 25 180a32–6.
[34] *Sophistical Refutations*, ch. 25, 180a35.
[35] See, e.g., Aquinas, *In III Sent.*, ed. Centre Traditio Litterarum Occidentalium, dist. 39.

3.6.2 Alius paralogismus quem ponit Aristoteles est iste: dicat Sortes contra mentem:

Ego sum mendax.

Aut mentitur aut non. Si mentitur, ergo dicit verum, ergo non mentitur. Si non mentitur, ergo dicit falsum, ergo mentitur. Pro quo est sciendum quod non solum mentitur qui dicit falsum, sed qui dicit verum contra mentem est mendax. Mentiri enim est contra mentem ire, unde qui unum credit in mente et aliud dicit ore mentitur etsi dicat verum, sicut patet de significato nominis. Dico ergo sicut dicit Aristoteles quod Sortes est mendax simpliciter, et cum arguitur: Ergo iurat verum quia iurat hoc solum, concedo. Et ideo est verus secundum quid | et simpliciter tamen mendax quia dicit illud verum contra mentem suam. Et sic solvit Aristoteles. E$_8$ 24vb

Si tamen solveretur sicut solvuntur insolubilia, non concederetur quod Sortes est mendax. Sed si ponatur quod 'mendax' et 'dicens falsum' convertuntur, tunc est ibi insolubile, et non debet concedi quod Sortes sit mendax, sicut patebit post. Hunc casum videtur Aristoteles concedere, et ideo constat quod hec non supponit Aristoteles, ut quidam putant.

3.6.3 Alius paralogismus quem ponit est iste: dissuadeat Sortes Platoni aliquid et suadeat eidem ut idem faciat, ergo illud simul suadet et dissuadet. Et solvitur quod suadere negationem non est suadere simpliciter sed secundum quid, et ideo simpliciter dissuadet et secundum quid suadet. Suadere enim est aliquem per verba allectiva ad aliquid concitare, et iste paralogismus manifeste non facit aliquid ad propositum.

3.7 Et ita patet quod Aristoteles huiusmodi insolubilia non solvit penes fallaciam secundum quid et simpliciter.

---

1 paralogismus] Secundus paralogismus *add. in marg.* E$_8$ ‖ est] *post* alius E$_4$ 2 contra] que E$_4$ 5 est sciendum] *inv.* E$_4$ 8 dicit] in *add.* E$_8$ 9 ergo] quod *add.* E$_8$ 10 et] *om.* E$_4$ ‖ Ergo] *om.* E$_4$ ‖ quia] qui E$_4$ 11 verus] verum E$_8$ 12 solvit Aristoteles] *inv.* E$_4$ 13 solveretur] solvantur E$_4$ 15 ibi] *om.* E$_4$ 16 casum *coniecimus*] causam *mss* ‖ et] *om.* E$_4$ 17 quidam] quedam E$_4$ 18 paralogismus] Tertius paralogismus *add. in marg.* E$_8$ ‖ quem ponit] *om.* E$_4$ 19 suadeat] suadeant E$_4$ ‖ idem] non *add.* E$_8$ ‖ faciat] faciant E$_4$ 20 suadere^2] *om.* E$_4$ 22 aliquem] aliquid E$_8$ ‖ concitare] contrarie E$_4$ 23 manifeste *corr.*] manifestum *mss*

3.6.2 Another paralogism which Aristotle presents is this:[36] let Socrates, contrary to his own mind, say:

> I am a liar.

Either he is lying or not. If he is lying then he speaks the truth, so he is not lying. If he is not lying, then he says a falsehood, so he is lying. Here it should be noted that not only one who says a falsehood is lying, but also one who speaks the truth contrary to his own mind is a liar. For to lie is to go against one's mind, and so anyone who believes one thing in his mind and says another with his mouth is lying even if he speaks the truth, as is clear from the meaning of the word.[37] I say, therefore, just as Aristotle says, that Socrates is unconditionally a liar; and when one argues: "therefore he swears a truth because he swears only this",[38] I grant it. And so he is conditionally truthful, but unconditionally a liar, because he speaks that truth contrary to his own mind. And this is how Aristotle solves it.

However, if one were to solve it as insolubles are solved, one would not grant that Socrates is a liar. But if it is claimed that 'liar' and 'saying a falsehood' are interchangeable, then there is an insoluble there, and it should not be granted that Socrates is a liar, as will be clear later. Aristotle seems to grant this scenario and so it is certain that Aristotle does not make these assumptions, as some people believe.

3.6.3 The other paralogism he presents is this: let Socrates dissuade Plato from something and persuade him to do the same thing, so he persuades and dissuades about it at the same time.[39] The solution is that persuading not, ⟨that is, dissuading from doing something,⟩ is not persuading unconditionally but conditionally, and so he dissuades unconditionally but persuades conditionally. For persuading someone is spurring him to do something by tempting words, and this paralogism manifestly does not say anything about that.

3.7 And thus it is clear that Aristotle does not solve insolubles of this sort by the fallacy of the conditional and the unconditional.

---

[36] *Sophistical Refutations*, 180b3–7; cf. Ockham, *Expositio super Libros Elenchorum*, II 10, §5.
[37] Segrave's suggested etymology here, reading 'mentire' (lying) as '(contra) ment(em) ire' (going against the mind), is found in, e.g., the twelfth-century *Derivationes* by Uguccione de Pisa (vol. I, M77 §13). On the claim that speaking against your own mind is lying, even if what you say is true, is found in Augustine's *De mendacio*, ed. Zycha, §3.
[38] *Sophistical Refutations*, 180b1.
[39] *De Sophisticis Elenchis*, tr. Boethius, 49: "Ergo possibile est eundem simul eidem suadere et dissuadere, aut non et esse quid et esse idem?"

Capitulum Quartum
⟨Solutio auctoris⟩

4.0 Istis premissis sine preiudicio aliorum dico quod omnia insolubilia solvenda sunt penes fallaciam accidentis. Dico quod isti sunt paralogismi difficillimi accidentis qui redarguunt sapientes, de quibus loquitur Aristoteles primo Elenchorum.

Pro quo sciendum est quod secundum fallaciam accidentis dupliciter fiunt paralogismi, vel ex variatione medii vel alterius extremorum: ex variatione medii ut si medium pro alio supponat in maiore quam faciat in minore vel pro alio supposito medii verificetur maior et minor; et ex variatione extremi similiter.

4.1 Dico ergo quod Sorte dicente:

    Sortes dicit falsum,

Sortes non dicit falsum.

4.1.1 Et cum arguitur:

    Hoc est falsum (demonstrato dicto a Sorte) | et Sortes E_8 25ra
    dicit hanc, ergo Sortes dicit falsum,

dico quod est fallacia accidentis ex variatione extremi. Iste enim terminus 'falsum' pro aliquo supponit in maiori pro quo non supponit in conclusione. Similiter si arguitur ex opposito dicti a Sorte:

    Nullum falsum dicitur a Sorte, hoc est falsum, ergo hoc
    non dicitur a Sorte,

hec est fallacia accidentis ex variatione medii; pro aliquo enim supponit iste terminus 'falsum' in minori pro quo non supponit in maiori. Sicut est de hoc paralogismo, ita est de omnibus similibus.

---

1 Capitulum Quartum] *in marg.* E_8 3 insolubilia] principaliter *add.* E_4 4–5 paralogismi] sillogismi E_4 7 est] *om.* E_4 9 alio] aliquo E_4 10 pro *corr.*] per E_8 || medii] *om.* E_4 10–11 ex variatione *corr.*] variationem *mss* 11 similiter] consimiliter E_4 15 cum] hoc *add.* E_4 16 dicto] dictum E_8 17 dicit[1]] dicat E_4 18 extremi] medii E_4 || enim] *om.* E_4 19 maiori *corr.*] minore *mss* 24 falsum] *om.* E_8

Chapter 4
⟨The author's solution⟩

4.0 Given these preliminaries, I say, without prejudging the views of others, that all insolubles ought to be solved by the fallacy of accident. I say that these are the most difficult paralogisms of accident, which confute the wise, of which Aristotle speaks in the first book of the *Sophistical Refutations*.[40]

Here one should be aware that according to the fallacy of accident paralogisms arise in two ways, either from variation of the middle term, or of one of the extremes: from variation of the middle if the middle term supposits for something else in the major premise than it does in the minor, or the major and minor are true for a different suppositum of the middle; and variation of an extreme is similar.

4.1 Hence I say that, if Socrates says:

Socrates says a falsehood,

Socrates does not say a falsehood.[41]

4.1.1 And when one argues:

This is a falsehood (referring to what was said by Socrates) and Socrates says this, hence Socrates says a falsehood,

I say that there is a fallacy of accident from variation of the extreme. For this term 'falsehood' supposits for something in the major premise for which it does not supposit in the conclusion. Similarly, if one argues from the opposite of what was said by Socrates:

No falsehood is said by Socrates, this is a falsehood, hence this is not said by Socrates,

this is a fallacy of accident by variation of the middle, for this term 'falsehood' supposits for something in the minor premise for which it does not supposit in the major.[42] Just as it is for this paralogism, so it is for all similar ones.

---

[40] *Sophistical Refutations* 6, 168a6–10.

[41] Both manuscripts read 'does not say' (*non dicit*). However, Paul of Venice (*Logica Magna: The Treatise on Insolubles*, ed. and tr. Bartocci and Read, §1.14.1.1), in his presentation of Segrave's solution, cites this passage almost verbatim, except that (in both the ms and the incunabulum) he attributes to Segrave the claim that if Socrates says only 'Socrates says a falsehood', then Socrates says a falsehood, and repeats this in his discussion at several points. The arguments that follow here show that Segrave's claim is that Socrates does not say a falsehood.

[42] Note that the major premise is the contradictory opposite of what was said by Socrates (in §4.1). So in the minor premise, both 'this' and 'falsehood' supposit for what was said by Socrates, but in the major premise, 'falsehood' cannot supposit for what was said by Socrates, by Segrave's principle, that no term can supposit for the opposite of the whole of which it is part. See also §6.8.1 and for further discussion, see Pozzi, *Il Mentitore e il Medioevo*, p. 59.

4.2 Sed quia recta solutio est manifestatio falsi sillogismi, oportet istam responsionem manifestare. Ad cuius manifestationem dico quod in nulla propositione supponit pars pro suo toto nec convertibili cum toto nec opposito totius nec antecedenti ad totum, ubi ex parte sic supponente sequitur evidenter totum esse falsum nisi forte fuerit propositio composita ex terminis repugnantibus, ex qua repugnantia terminorum expressam contradictionem claudit, ut hec:

    Quodlibet impossibile est possibile.

Sed de talibus nihil ad presens.

4.3 Istam propositionem probare volumus, et illius causam demonstrare est totam responsionem manifestare, pro quo premictam unam diffinitionem eius quod dico 'supponere' et unam aliam suppositionem ex qua sequitur intentum.

⟨Diffinitio suppositionis⟩

4.4 Pro quo sciendum ⟨est⟩ quod non quodlibet significare termini est ipsum supponere. ⟨Terminus⟩ significat enim in oratione, et extra contextum non supponit sed suppositionem habet ex hoc quod est pars propositionis. Nec etiam quodlibet significatum eius in propositione supponitur, quia sic dicendo:

    Animal rationale est homo,

li 'animal' quodlibet animal significat, sed tantum hominem supponit. Supponere ergo pro aliquo est significare ipsum extremum unionis significate per copulam. Et 'est' in propositionibus, ut dicitur in libro Peryarmenias, significat quamdam compositionem mentalem quam sine | extremis non est intelligere. Et ista compositio mentalis significat compositionem talem esse ex parte rei et similiter divisio mentalis negativa significat talem divisionem in re. Extrema igitur propositionis suppositionem capiunt a tali copulatione. Supponere pro suis suppositis est significare illa esse extrema illius unionis ex parte rei quam significat copula. Et hoc faciunt aliquando copulative aliquando disiunctive, secundum quod diversum modum supponendi habent ex adiunctis.

E₈ 25rb

---

1 solutio] solutione *a.c.* solutio *p.c.* E₈   4 ubi] quia E₄   ‖ sic] sit E₈   ‖ supponente] suppositio E₄ supponere E₈   5 forte] *om.* E₄   6-7 expressam contradictionem] expressam contradictio E₄   9 Sed] *om.* E₄   16 contextum] conceptum (*dub.*) E₈   17 suppositionem] non *add.* E₄   ‖ hoc] quod E₄   18 eius] *om.* E₄   ‖ quia] si *add.* E₄   21 hominem] *om.* E₄   22 ergo] autem *add.* E₄   22-23 significate] significare E₄   23 Et est] est enim E₄   25 significat] quandam *add.* E₈   26 talem¹] unionem *add.* E₈   ‖ mentalis] etiam *add.* E₈   28 copulatione *corr.*] copulativa *mss*   ‖ esse] *om.* E₄   29-30 faciunt aliquando] *inv.* E₄   30 aliquando] *om.* E₄

4.2 But because the correct solution is the exhibition[43] of a false syllogism, it is necessary to exhibit this response. For its exhibition I say that in no proposition does a part supposit for its whole (nor for what is convertible with the whole nor for the opposite of the whole nor for what implies the whole), where from the part suppositing in this way it clearly follows that the whole is false—unless perhaps the proposition were composed of inconsistent terms and from the inconsistency of those terms it includes an express contradiction, e.g.,

>Everything impossible is possible.

But such cases are not relevant to our present concerns.

4.3 We want to prove this claim, and showing its cause is to exhibit the whole response, for which I shall put forth my own definition of 'supposit' and one other postulate from which what is wanted follows.

⟨Definition of supposition⟩

4.4 To this end it should be noted that not every signifying of a term is its suppositing. For ⟨a term⟩ signifies in an utterance, and outside the context ⟨of an utterance⟩ it does not supposit but ⟨only⟩ has supposition from being part of a proposition. Nor even is every one of its significates supposited ⟨for⟩ in a proposition. Because, saying this:

>A rational animal is a man,

'animal' signifies every animal, but only supposits ⟨for⟩ a man.[44] Therefore, to supposit for something is to signify an extreme of the union signified by the copula. And 'is' in propositions, as is said in the *Perihermeneias*, signifies some mental composition which is not comprehensible without the extremes.[45] And this mental composition signifies that there is such composition in reality, and similarly, mental division and a negative proposition signify such division in things. Therefore, the extremes of a proposition take supposition from such a coupling. To supposit for its supposita is to signify them to be the extremes of that union in reality which the copula signifies. They do this sometimes conjunctively, sometimes disjunctively, insofar as they receive a different mode of suppositing from what is adjoined to them.

---

[43] See §3.4 above.
[44] The supposition of 'man' is restricted by the adjoining of 'rational'. See §ad 5.4 below.
[45] Aristotle, *De Interpretatione*, ch. 3, 16b24 (tr. Boethius, p. 7, 18–19); Hamesse, *Les Auctoritates Aristotelis*, p. 305, # 7.

⟨Suppositio de significatione⟩

4.5 Suppositio est hec: quod quelibet propositio denotat ita esse ex parte rei sicut ⟨ipsa⟩ significat. Hec est manifesta per se et patet per philosophum et commentatorem 5° metaphysice commento 14 et in littera illius commenti per totum, copula enim in propositione significat esse verum, ut ibi declarabitur.

4.5.1 Ex hac sequitur alia quod quelibet propositio non includens contradictionem significat ita esse ex parte rei sicut ipsa significat, et non significat ita non esse, quia si significaret illa duo expressam contradictionem includeret, quod est contra ypotesim.

4.5.2 Ex hac sequitur demonstrative propositum sic: quelibet propositio non includens contradictionem significat ita esse ex parte rei sicut ipsa significat, et non significat ita non esse; sed ita esse ex parte rei sicut ipsa propositio significat et non ita non esse est propositionem esse veram et non falsam, et hoc si illa propositio est; ergo quelibet propositio non includens contradictionem, cum hoc quod ipsa est, significat se esse veram et non falsam.

Et hoc patet de qualibet propositione inductive. Sequitur enim:

> Ita est ex parte rei in toto sicut significat ista 'tu sedes', et hec est, ergo hec est vera et non falsa,

et ita de aliis. Ergo quelibet propositio non includens contradictionem, cum hoc quod ipsa est, significat se esse | veram et non falsam. E₄ 160ra

4.5.3 Ex hac | sequitur ulterius quod extrema propositionis tantum illa supponunt pro quibus totum potest denotare se esse verum, cum hoc quod ipsum est, et non supponunt talia pro quibus totum, cum hoc quod ipsum est, denotaret se esse falsum. Et hoc est propositum. In ista ergo: E₈ 25va

---

8 esse] *om.* E₈ ‖ ipsa] propositio E₄   9 non] *om.* E₄   8–11 et non significat ... propositio] *in marg.* E₄   12 ipsa] propositio E₄   13 esse² *corr.*] est E₈ *om.* E₄   13–14 non significat ... et non] *om.* E₄   14 esse¹] *om.* E₄ ‖ est propositionem] *iter. et del.* E₈   15 si] in E₄   19 in toto] note E₈   20 hec¹ *corr.*] hoc E₄ homo E₈ ‖ ergo] *om.* E₈ ‖ hec²] hoc E₄   22 falsam] et *add.* E₄   25 cum] *om.* E₈

⟨A postulate about signification⟩

4.5 The postulate is this: that every proposition means things being in reality as it signifies. This is self-evident and is clear from the Philosopher and the Commentator in comment 14 on the fifth book of the *Metaphysics* and throughout the text of that comment:[46] for the copula in the proposition signifies being true, as elucidated there.

4.5.1 From this it follows further that every proposition not involving a contradiction signifies things being in reality as it signifies, and does not signify things not being ⟨in reality as it signifies⟩, because if it signified them both it would involve an express contradiction, which is contrary to the hypothesis.

4.5.2 From this, what was claimed follows ostensively in this way: every proposition not involving a contradiction signifies things being in reality as it signifies, and does not signify things not being ⟨in reality as it signifies⟩. But things being in reality as the proposition signifies, and not things not being ⟨in reality as it signifies⟩ is for a proposition to be true and not false, provided the proposition exists; so every proposition not involving a contradiction, assuming it exists, signifies itself to be true and not false.

And this is clear of every proposition one by one. For this inference is valid:

> Things are in reality wholly as the proposition 'You are sitting' signifies, and it exists, therefore this proposition is true and not false,

and the same is true of other propositions. Therefore, every proposition not involving a contradiction, assuming it exists, signifies itself to be true and not false.[47]

4.5.3 From this it follows further that the extremes of a proposition only supposit ⟨for⟩ those things about which the whole can mean that it itself is true, assuming that it exists, and those extremes do not supposit ⟨for⟩ those things about which the whole, assuming that it exists, would mean that it itself is false. And this is what I claim. Therefore, in this:

---

[46] See *Aristotelis opera cum Averrois commentaria*, vol. VIII *In Metaphysicen* V 7, de ente, comm. 14 f. 117E: https://archive.org/details/bub_gb_u_T0u0IuuyIC/page/n251/mode/2up (ed. Ponzalli, pp. 131–32), commenting on Aristotle's text at 1017a31–35.

[47] Note that in this argument, Segrave implicitly appeals to Bradwardine's famous second postulate (Bradwardine, *Insolubilia*, §6.3): "Every proposition signifies or means as a matter of fact or absolutely everything which follows from it as a matter of fact or absolutely" (quelibet propositio significat sive denotat ut nunc vel simpliciter omne quod sequitur ad istam ut nunc vel simpliciter). Segrave's disagreement with Bradwardine is over his third postulate: "The part can supposit for its whole and for its opposite and for what is equivalent to them" (pars potest supponere pro suo toto et eius opposito et convertibilibus earundem), which Segrave explicitly denied at §4.2.

> Falsum est

non supponit subiectum pro toto quia tunc posset denotare se esse verum pro se falso sine contradictione, quod tamen est falsum quia hoc esse verum pro se falso includit contradictionem.

4.6 Ideo forte dicitur quod hec:

> Falsum est,

et quelibet consimilis ubi cadit insolubile, includit contradictionem aliquo casu posito.

ad 4.6 Sed istud nihil est quia ista propositio non significat illum casum poni nec esse verum, quia secundum sic dicentes

> Falsum est

non significat se esse falsum nisi ipso existente et nullo alio falso. Sed manifestum est quod ista:

> Falsum est

non significat nullum aliud falsum esse. Semper enim uno modo significat quantum est ex parte sua, cum non sit agens cognoscens, sicut primum argutum est.

4.6.1 Sed forte dicitur quod non sequitur:

> A non significat nullum aliud falsum esse, ergo non significat se esse falsum.

ad 4.6.1 Sed contra: ista consequentia est necessaria:

> A est falsum, ergo nullum aliud falsum ab A est,

quia si foret aliud falsum, tunc A esset verum, ergo quicquid infert vel significat antecedens significat consequens, ergo, ex opposito, quod non significat consequens non significat antecedens.

4.6.2 Sed dicis: ista iam dicta bene probant quod ita est quod pars non supponit pro toto nec convertibili et ita de aliis, sed non dicunt causam quare | ita est.

ad 4.6.2 Et dico quod causa patet ex predictis et est hec: quia extrema suppositionem capiunt a copula cuius significatum est esse verum, ut dictum est, ideo non supponit pro aliquo pro quo totum denotaret se

---

3 falso *corr.*] falsa *mss.*   5 hec] hoc E$_4$ 12 falsum] falsam E$_4$ || nullo alio] *inv.* E$_4$ 12–13 sed manifestum ... ista] in quantum est ex parte sui E$_4$ 15 Semper enim uno] enim semper opposito E$_4$ 16 quantum ... sua] *om.* E$_4$ 18 Sed] *om.* E$_4$ 21 ista consequentia] *inv.* E$_8$ 26 dicis] dicet E$_4$ || probant] probat E$_8$ 30 suppositionem capiunt] *inv.* E$_4$ 31 denotaret] denotat E$_4$

> A falsehood exists,

the subject does not supposit for the whole because then it could mean that it itself is true about its false self without contradiction, which, however, is false because 'being true about its false self' involves a contradiction.

4.6 For this reason one might perhaps say that this:

> A falsehood exists,

and every similar proposition where an insoluble occurs, involves a contradiction in some assumed scenario.

ad 4.6 But this cannot be right because this proposition does not signify that this scenario is assumed nor that it is true, because according to those advocating this solution,

> A falsehood exists

does not signify that it itself is a falsehood except when it exists and no other falsehood exists. But it is evident that this:

> A falsehood exists,

does not signify that no other falsehood exists. For it always signifies in one way for its own part, since it does not have a mind of its own, as was argued earlier.[48]

4.6.1 But perhaps one can say that this inference is not valid:

> A does not signify that no other falsehood exists, so it does not signify that it itself is false.

ad 4.6.1 But on the contrary: this inference is necessary:

> A is false, therefore no other falsehood than A exists,

because if there were another falsehood, then A would be true, so whatever implies or signifies the premise signifies the conclusion,[49] so from the opposite, the premise does not signify what the conclusion does not signify.

4.6.2 But you object: what has already been said confirms that the part does not supposit for the whole nor for what is convertible with it, and so on, but they do not give a reason why this is.

ad 4.6.2 I say that the reason is clear from what has been said, and it is because the extremes take their supposition from the copula, whose significate is that the proposition is true, as was said. So the extreme

---

[48] See §2.2.8.

[49] If it were not for the implicit appeal to Bradwardine's second postulate in §4.5 (see n. 36) one might suspect that his use of it here was ad hominem, since he is here presumably arguing against Bradwardine. Bradwardine would presumably concede that A does signify that no other falsehood than A exists, since that follows from the claim that A is false.

esse falsum vel non esse verum, quia hoc repugnaret significato copule et ideo restringantur per copulativam rationem. Unde hec opinio dicta est opinio restringentium. Aliquando tamen accidit quod extrema supponunt contrarium illius quod significatur per copulam et hoc accidit ex repugnantia extremorum ad invicem vel ex aliqua repugnantia inclusa in altero extremorum.

Sic igitur patet quia est et propter quid est.

4.7 Istud idem potest aliter probari sic supponendo cum philosopho quod ex universali contingit inferri quodlibet pro quo subiectum supponit, super hoc enim dependet omnis evidentia sillogistica, sicut patet primo Priorum. Ex hoc sequitur quod ex singulari contingit inferre suam particularem ubi supponit pro illa singulari.

4.7.1 Hiis positis, partem non supponere pro suo toto et hoc in talibus ubi si faceret sequeretur ipsam esse falsam sequitur ex utraque parte contradictionis cum istis positionibus iam suppositis. Hoc arguo sic: Sequitur

---

2 restringantur] restringatur E_4 4 illius] illo E_4 5 inclusa] inclusi E_8 7 quia] quare E_8 8 Istud] illud E_4 10 super hoc] semper E_4 14 sequeretur] sequitur E_4 15 iam suppositis] *inv.* E_4 16 Sequitur] sequeretur E_8

does not supposit for anything about which the whole would mean that it itself is false or is not true, because this would be inconsistent with the significate of the copula, and so the extremes should be restricted by the meaning of the copula. So this solution[50] is called the solution of the restrictivists. Sometimes, however, it happens that the extremes supposit for the contrary of what is signified by the copula, and this results from the mutual inconsistency of the extremes or from some inconsistency involved in one of the extremes.

In this way, therefore, it is clear that ⟨the part does not supposit for its whole⟩ and why.[51]

4.7 That same ⟨claim, *viz* that the part does not supposit for its whole where it would mean that it itself is false⟩ can be proved in another way by assuming with Aristotle that from a universal proposition one can infer anything for which the subject supposits, since the evidential force of all syllogistic reasoning depends on this assumption,[52] as is clear from the first book of the *Prior Analytics*. From this it follows that from a singular proposition one can infer the corresponding particular proposition where ⟨the subject⟩ supposits for that singular.[53]

4.7.1 With these assumptions in place, ⟨the claim⟩ that the part does not supposit for its whole in cases where if it did it would follow that it was false follows from each member of a contradictory pair with the assumptions already assumed.[54] I argue for it like this: the inference

---

[50] That is, Segrave's own solution.

[51] Segrave is alluding here to the distinction between two forms of explanation: quia et propter quid (the reason and the reason why). See Aristotle, *Posterior Analytics* I 13, and, e.g., Longeway, 'Medieval Theories of Demonstration', §1.

[52] Presumably what Segrave is referring to here is the dici de omni et nullo: *Prior Analytics*, I 1, 24b29–32.

[53] If from 'All A is/is not B' we can infer 'This A is/is not B', then by contraposition, from 'This A is not/is B' (equivalently, 'This A is/is not B') we can infer 'Some A is not/is B' (equivalently, 'Some A is/is not B').

[54] The structure of the argument to follow is proof by cases from an instance of the Law of Excluded Middle (LEM), whose parts constitute a contradictory pair. By LEM, either the subject of A supposits for A or the subject of A does not supposit for A. Suppose the subject of A supposits for A, where A is 'A falsehood exists'. Then by the contrapositive of the *dici de nullo*, from 'This falsehood ⟨*viz* A⟩ exists' we can infer 'A falsehood exists' ⟨that is, A⟩, so A is true, so A is not false, and so the subject of A does not supposit for A. But clearly, if the subject of A does not supposit for A then the subject of A does not supposit for A. So either way, the subject of A does not supposit for A. (Another way of construing this proof is as an instance of consequentia mirabilis: if p then not-p, so not-p. See, e.g., Kneale, 'Aristotle and the Consequentia Mirabilis'.) The proof then needs to be generalized in order to conclude that, quite generally, the part cannot supposit for the whole. Moreover, the derivation of not-p from p (i.e., if the subject of A supposits for A then the subject of A does not supposit for A') seems to depend on previously showing that A is false. So Segrave seems to accept the standard argument that an insoluble, if true, is false, and so is false; but rejects the further argument that if false, it's true, inferring from the contradiction (that otherwise it would be both true and false) that the subject of A does not supposit for A. That move is usually rejected as being ad hoc, in the absence of any explanation why the subject of A does not supposit for A.

> In ista 'falsum est', subiectum non supponit pro toto, ergo subiectum non supponit pro toto.

Ista consequentia, etsi sit petitio principii, necessaria est quia arguitur ab eodem ad idem, et hoc sufficit ad propositum.

4.7.2 Sequitur ex alia cum aliis | veris positis quod non supponit. Hoc probo sic: si subiectum supponat pro A, sit A totum, ergo sequitur:

> A, est ergo falsum est,

per suppositum, quia singularis infert suam particularem, et antecedens in hac consequentia est verum, ergo consequens est verum. Et sequitur ultra: hoc consequens est verum, ergo non supponit pro A.

4.7.3 Ergo a primo, ex utraque parte contradictionis cum quibusdam veris alteri parti additis sequitur partem ipsius A non supponere pro A. Ultima consequentia patet quia subiectum A non supponit nisi pro falsis, cum sit iste terminus 'falsum'.

4.7.4 Dicitur forte quod non sequitur:

> Partem ipsius A non supponere pro A sequitur ex utraque parte contradictionis cum quibusdam additis veris alteri parti contradictionis, ergo partem A non supponere pro A est verum,

quia potest esse quod illa vera repugnant illi parti cui adduntur.

ad 4.7.4 Contra: illud non vetat sive prohibet quia ex hac parte contradictionis:

> Pars A non supponit pro A,

sequitur partem A non supponere pro A et hoc absque alio vero addito. Si igitur vera addita alteri parti repugnant illi, cum verum vero non repugnet, ergo ista pars contradictionis est falsa, ergo hec est falsa:

> Pars A supponit pro A,

ergo eius oppositum est verum:

---

1 est] falsum *add.* E_8 2 toto] tota E_8 3 petitio principii] *inv.* E_4 ‖ arguitur] argumenta E_4 4 et] *om.* E_4 ‖ propositum] et *add.* E_4 7 A] *scr. et del.* E_8 ‖ est^2] *om.* E_4 9 consequentia] antecedens *add.* E_4 12 alteri] alteri *vel* alicui (*dub.*) *p.c.* E_8 ‖ parti] particulariter E_8 ‖ A^2] alia E_4 13 falsis] falsa (*dub.*) E_4 14 terminus] *om.* E_4 15 forte] a Sorte E_4 *a.c.*E_8 20 vera] prima E_8 ‖ repugnant *corr.*] repugnat *mss* 25 vero] *post* repugnet E_4 27 A^1] non *add. mss*

> The subject of 'A falsehood exists' does not supposit for
> the whole, so the subject does not supposit for the whole,

even if it begs the question, holds of necessity because it proceeds from the same to the same, and this is enough for my purposes.

4.7.2 That ⟨the subject⟩ does not supposit ⟨for the whole⟩ follows from the other ⟨part of the contradictory pair⟩ with other truths in place. I prove it like this: if the subject ⟨of 'A falsehood exists'⟩ supposits for A, where A is the whole, then

> A exists, therefore a falsehood exists

is valid (by assumption because a singular proposition implies the corresponding particular), and the premise in this inference is true, so the conclusion is true. And given that the conclusion is true, it follows that ⟨the subject⟩ does not supposit for A.[55]

4.7.3 Therefore from the beginning, that is, from each part of a contradictory pair with certain truths added to one part, it follows that part of A does not supposit for A. The last inference is clear because the subject of A supposits only for falsehoods, since it is this term 'falsehood'.

4.7.4 But perhaps someone objects that this is invalid:

> That part of A does not supposit for A follows from each
> part of the contradictory pair with certain truths added
> to one part of the contradictory pair, therefore it is true
> that part of A does not supposit for A,

because it can be that those truths are inconsistent with the part to which they are added.[56]

ad 4.7.4 On the contrary: that does not block the argument, because from this part of the contradictory pair:

> Part of A does not supposit for A,

it follows that part of A does not supposit for A, and it does so without another truth added. Therefore, if the truths added to the other part are inconsistent with it, since truth is not inconsistent with truth, then this part of the contradiction is false, so this is false:

> Part of A supposits for A,

therefore, its opposite is true:

---

[55] For we have just proved that A is true—as Segrave himself explains in the last sentence of the paragraph.
[56] The objection seems to be that what is added to one part of the contradictory pair might be inconsistent with that part, so the premises as a whole would be false, and so would not warrant inferring the conclusion. The reply will be that the addition was of truths, and it was only added to the affirmative part of the contradictory pair, so that part must be false and we have what we wanted.

Nulla pars A supponit pro A;
et ita semper sequitur quod pars A non supponit pro A. | E₈ 26rb

Capitulum Quintum

⟨Obiectiones contra positionem auctoris et responsiones eiusdem⟩

5.0 Contra istam positionem arguitur multipliciter. Primo contra hoc quod ponitur quod pars non supponit pro toto nec opposito totius, ubi partem sic supponere sequitur totum esse falsum.

5.1 Primo per auctoritatem Aristotelis: 4° Metaphysice in fine dicit Aristoteles sic arguendo contra illos qui posuerunt omnia ⟨esse⟩ vera et illos qui posuerunt omnia ⟨esse⟩ falsa:

> Accidit et quod est famatum de omnibus talibus orationibus ⟨ipsas⟩ se ipsas destruere. Nam qui omnia vera dicit, orationis sue contrariam veram facit, quare eiusdem non veram; contraria enim non dicit ⟨ipsam esse veram⟩. Qui vero omnia falsa et se ipsum.

Ex hac auctoritate videtur quod subiectum in ista:

> Omnia sunt vera,

supponit pro eius opposito, ex quo tamen sequitur hanc esse falsam. Similiter hic:

> Omnia sunt falsa,

subiectum supponit pro toto, ex quo tamen sequitur totum esse falsum.

5.2 Secundo arguitur sic: Idem est subiectum huius:

> Falsum est,

et predicatum huius:

> Hoc ⟨est⟩ falsum,

demonstrato: 'falsum est', et hoc intellectu, quia aliter recipiens non denudaretur a natura recepti. Sed predicatum huius:

---

2 supponit] supponat E₈   3 Capitulum Quintum] *in marg.* E₈   8 partem] ex parte E₄   12 et] *om.* E₄ || famatum de *corr.*] factum *mss* || talibus] *om.* E₄   15 contraria *corr.* – *vide Moerbeke tr.*] contrariam *mss*   19 quo] qua E₈   22 totum esse falsum] quod totum est falsum E₄   23 huius] hoc E₄   27 hoc] hec E₈   28 recepti] rei recepte E₄

No part of A supposits for A;

and thus it follows either way that part of A does not supposit for A.

Chapter 5
⟨Objections to the author's solution and his replies⟩

5.0 One may argue against this solution in numerous ways. First of all, ⟨one may argue⟩ against the claim that a part does not supposit for its whole nor for the opposite of the whole, where from the part suppositing in this way it follows that the whole is false.[57]

5.1 First, by the authority of Aristotle: in *Metaphysics* Γ 8, when he argues against those claiming that everything is true and those claiming that everything is false, Aristotle says:

> "And, as is widely known, it happens that all such utterances destroy themselves. For one who says that everything is true, makes the contrary of his own utterance true and so makes his own utterance not true, for the utterance contrary ⟨to his own⟩ denies ⟨that it is true⟩. However, one who ⟨says⟩ that everything is false, ⟨says it⟩ of himself."[58]

From this authoritative passage it appears that the subject of this proposition:

Everything is true,

supposits for its opposite, from which, however, it follows that this proposition is false. Similarly, here:

Everything is false,

the subject supposits for the whole, from which, however, it follows that the whole is false.

5.2 Secondly, one ⟨may⟩ argue like this: the subject of

A falsehood exists

and the predicate of

This ⟨is⟩ a falsehood,

referring to 'A falsehood exists', are the same in the mind, because otherwise the receiver would not have been stripped of the nature of what was received.[59] But the predicate of

---

[57] Cf. §4.2.
[58] See Aristotle, *Metaphysica*, tr. Moerbeke, p. 91; Aristotle, *Metaphysics*, Γ 8, 1012b14–18, Cf. Bradwardine, *Insolubilia*, §§3.1.1 and 3.2.1.

> Hoc est falsum,

supponit pro A (sit A ista: Falsum est), ergo subiectum ipsius A supponit pro A.

5.3 Preterea: sic dicto:

> Aliquid est,

vel:

> Verum est,

subiectum supponit pro toto, ergo ⟨similiter⟩ sic dicto:

> Falsum est,

vel:

> Nullum verum est.

5.4 Preterea: pars A significat totum A (sit A: falsum est), ergo potest supponere pro A eadem ratione quod significat totum. Patet quia idem significat in oratione et extra, sed extra A significat A, ergo in A significat A. |

5.5 Preterea: ista vox B significat se ipsam, ergo B multo fortius potest significare totum hoc:

> B est falsum,

et hoc cum voces sint ad placitum; potest ergo Sortes velle B ita significare | et ita significabit.

5.6 Preterea: sic dicto:

> Nullum falsum dicitur a Sorte,

hic est dici de nullo, ergo nihil contingit sumere sub subiecto quin ab eo removeatur terminus predicatus, et si sic per ipsum denotatur predicatum removeri ab hoc 'falsum', demonstrato hoc

> Falsum dicitur a Sorte,

cum ista contineatur sub subiecto.

---

2 ista] est *add.* E$_4$ || subiectum] *om.* E$_4$ 3 pro] per E$_4$ 8 pro] A *add.* E$_8$ 14 in^2] oratione *add.* E$_4$ || A^3] sic *add.* E$_4$ 16 B^1] A E$_8$ || B^2] A E$_8$ 23 hic] hoc E$_4$ 24 terminus predicatus] quare cuius(*dub.*) terminus(*dub.*) E$_4$ || et] *om.* E$_4$ 25 falsum *corr.*] falso *mss*   26 Falsum] falso E$_8$

> This is a falsehood

supposits for A (where A is 'A falsehood exists'),[60] therefore the subject of A supposits for A.

5.3 Moreover:[61] if one says:

> Something exists

or

> A truth exists,

the subject supposits for the whole, therefore ⟨so too⟩ if one says:

> A falsehood exists

or

> No truth exists.

5.4 Moreover:[62] a part of A signifies the whole of A (where A is 'A falsehood exists'), therefore, ⟨a part of A⟩ can supposit for ⟨the whole of⟩ A for the same reason that it signifies the whole. This is clear because it signifies the same thing placed within and outside an utterance, but placed outside of A it signifies A, therefore placed within A it signifies A.

5.5 Moreover:[63] the expression B signifies itself, therefore *a fortiori* B can signify the whole:

> B is a falsehood,

and this is possible since expressions are at the pleasure ⟨of the impositor⟩; therefore Socrates can wish that B signifies in this way and it will signify in this way.

5.6 Moreover:[64] if one says:

> No falsehood is said by Socrates,

here we have the *dici de nullo*,[65] therefore nothing can be taken under the subject without removing the predicate term from it. And if so, it means that the predicate is removed from 'falsehood' referring to this:

> A falsehood is said by Socrates,

since this proposition is contained under the subject.

---

[59] Averroes, *On the Soul*, Γ, comm. 4 (*Commentarium Magnum in Aristotelis De Anima Libros*, ed. Crawford, 385–86); Hamesse, *Les Auctoritates Aristotelis*, p. 191, n. 212; Aristotle, *On the Soul*, Γ, 4, 429a15–23. Cf. Bradwardine, *Insolubilia*, §3.1.3.
[60] At long last Segrave says what he's taken A to be ever since §ad 4.6.1.
[61] Cf. Bradwardine, *Insolubilia*, §3.1.4.
[62] Cf. Bradwardine, *Insolubilia*, §3.2.3.
[63] Cf. Bradwardine, *Insolubilia*, §3.1.6.
[64] Cf. Bradwardine, *Insolubilia*, §3.1.7.
[65] See n. 14.

5.7 Preterea: hec exceptiva est vera:

> Nullum falsum preter A dicitur a Sorte.

Sit A hoc 'falsum dicitur a Sorte'. Queritur ergo utrum subiectum preiacentis supponat pro A vel non. Si sic, habetur propositum. Si non, ergo non est ibi extra captio partis a toto, ergo non exceptiva.

Preterea: in omni exceptiva preiacens repugnat exceptive, quod non est verum in proposito nisi in preiacente subiectum supponat pro A.

5.8.1 Preterea: subiectum huius:

> Falsum est

(que sit B) supponit pro ista:

> Falsum est dictum a Sorte

(que sit A). Sed idem est subiectum B et A, ergo subiectum ipsius A supponit pro A.

5.8.2 Aliter sic: isti duo termini convertuntur: 'falsum', et: 'hoc falsum vel illud et sic de singulis', ergo de quocumque vere predicatur unus, vere predicatur et reliquus. Sed hec est vera:

> Sortes dicit hoc falsum vel illud et sic de singulis,

ergo erit hec vera:

> Sortes dicit falsum.

Similiter si convertuntur, pro quocumque potest unus terminus supponere potest alius supponere.

5.9 Ultimo sic: si tales paralogismi solvendi essent secundum accidens, cum non sit verisimile tales latuisse Aristotelem, ergo solvisset tales paralogismos secundum accidens ubi ergo solvit illos.

Ad ista respondeo faciliter.

---

5 ibi] *om.* E_4 ‖ extra captio] excipi E_4 8–9 huius ... est] hoc est falsum E_4 10 supponit] supponat E_8 12 B *corr.*] *om. mss*   16 et] *om.* E_4 18 hec] *om.* E_4 19 falsum] *om.* E_4 20 terminus] *om.* E_4 23 sit] sint E_8 ‖ tales[1]] *om.* E_4 ‖ ergo solvisset] vel solvisse E_4 25 respondeo] respondetur E_4

5.7 Moreover:[66] this exceptive is true:

> No falsehood except A is said by Socrates.

Let A be 'A falsehood is said by Socrates'. It is then asked if the subject of the prejacent[67] ⟨sc. 'No Falsehood is said by Socrates'⟩ supposits for A or not. If so, we have what we claimed. If not, then here there is no excepting of a part from the whole, therefore it is not an exceptive.

Moreover: in every exceptive, the prejacent is incompatible with the exceptive, which is not true in the above case unless in the prejacent the subject supposits for A.

5.8.1 Moreover:[68] the subject of

> A falsehood exists,

call it B, supposits for

> A falsehood is said by Socrates,

call it A. But the subject of B and of A is the same, therefore the subject of A supposits for A.

5.8.2 ⟨One can argue⟩ in another way like this: the two terms 'falsehood' and 'this falsehood or that and so on for every instance' are convertible, therefore of anything of which one is truly predicated the other is truly predicated as well. But this is true:

> Socrates says this falsehood or that and so on for every instance,

therefore this will be true:

> Socrates says a falsehood.

Similarly, if they are convertible, one term can supposit for anything for which the other can supposit.

5.9 Finally, ⟨one can argue⟩ like this: if these paralogisms were to be solved by the fallacy of accident, then since it not likely that they passed unnoticed by Aristotle, he would have solved such paralogisms, where he does solve them, by the fallacy of accident.

I easily respond to these arguments.

---

[66] Cf. Bradwardine, *Insolubilia*, §3.2.2.
[67] See Paul of Venice, *Logica Magna*, f. 38ra: "The prejacent of an exceptive is said to be what remains with the exceptive word and the excepted part removed" (Preiacens exceptive dicitur esse illud quod remanet dempta dictione exceptiva cum parte extra capta). More generally, 'prejacent' seems to have been used to refer to the unmodified form of a modal or similar proposition: see, e.g., Ockham, 'Modal Consequences' (*Summa Logicae*, III-3 ch. 10, 13) in Kretzmann and Stump, *The Cambridge Translations of Medieval Philosophical Texts*, vol. I, pp. 320, 329.
[68] Cf. Bradwardine, *Insolubilia*, §3.2.4.

ad 5.1 Ad primum dico quod Aristoteles ibi arguit contra Eraclitum | E₈ 26vb
qui posuit omnia aliquando esse in motu et tunc omnia ⟨esse⟩ falsa, et
aliquando omnia in quiete et tunc omnia esse vera; et contra illos est
argumentum bonum, quia ex eadem causa habent hii dicere quod hec
est falsa:

    Omnia sunt falsa,

sicut eius oppositum. Et hoc est quod dicit Commentator quod isti dicunt
quod omnia opposita sunt vera et omnia opposita sunt falsa. Et similiter
qui dicunt omnia esse vera quia aliquando sunt in quiete omnia, habent
dicere ex eadem causa quod oppositum huius est verum, non quia in ista:

    Quodlibet est verum,

subiectum supponat pro eius opposito, sed quia ex eadem ratione qua
dicunt unum esse verum, debent dicere eius oppositum esse verum. Et
ista auctoritas sic intellecta nihil facit ad propositum nec contra dicta.

ad 5.2 Ad aliud conceditur quod eadem intentio est subiectum huius:

    Falsum est,

et predicatum huius:

    Hoc est falsum.

Et nego consequentiam:

    Ergo si predicatum huius: Hoc est falsum, supponit pro
    A, ergo subiectum ipsius A supponit pro A et hoc in
    ipso A.

Bene potest esse quod illa | intentio,* que est subiectum A, in alia propos-   O 1ra
itione supponat ⟨pro A⟩.

ad 5.8.1 Et per hoc solvitur unum aliud argumentum videlicet quod etsi
idem est subiectum huius:

    Falsum est,

et:

    Falsum est dictum a Sorte,

non tamen sequitur quod respectu istorum diversorum predicatorum
supponat pro eodem vel in respectu diverse copule.

*Incipit ms O

---

1 ibi] ubi E₈   8 opposita¹] *om.* E₄   9 omnia²] *om.* E₄   10 quia] quod E₄   12 subiectum supponat] *inv.* E₄ || quia] quod E₄   13 Et] etiam E₈   14 sic] recto E₄ est *add.* E₈ || ad ... nec] *om.* E₄   21 et] in *add.* E₄ || hoc] hic E₈   23 alia] alio E₄   24 supponat] supponit O   25 videlicet] scilicet O || etsi] si E₄ O   29 dictum] tantum *add.* O   30 quod] in *add.* O

ad 5.1 To the first argument: I say that here Aristotle is arguing against Heraclitus, who claimed that sometimes everything is in movement and so everything ⟨is⟩ false, and sometimes everything is at rest and so everything is true. And the argument is valid against those people, because for the very same reason they have to say that this is false:

> Everything is false,

just as its opposite is. And this is what the Commentator says: that they say that all opposites are true and all opposites are false.[69] And similarly, those who say that everything is true because sometimes everything is at rest, for the same reason they have to say that its opposite is true, not because in

> Everything is true

the subject supposits for its opposite, but because for the same reason for which they say that the one is true they have to say that its opposite is true. And understood in this way this authoritative passage is irrelevant for our purposes nor does it go against what was claimed.

ad 5.2 To the next argument: I grant that the same intention[70] is the subject of

> A falsehood exists

and the predicate of

> This is a falsehood.

And I deny that one can validly infer:

> therefore if the predicate of 'This is a falsehood' supposits for A ⟨sc. 'A falsehood exists'⟩, then the subject of A supposits for A, and this in A itself.

It can well be the case that the intention which is the subject of A supposits ⟨for A⟩ in another proposition.

ad 5.8.1 And another argument is solved by this, namely that although the subject of

> A falsehood exists

and

> A falsehood is said by Socrates

is the same, yet it does not follow that with respect to these different predicates or with respect to a different copula the subject supposits for the same thing.

---

[69] Averroes, *On Metaphysics*, Γ 8, comm. 29 (in Averroes, *Aristotelis Metaphysicorum libri XIIII cum Averrois Commentariis*, f. 99E–M: https://archive.org/details/bub_gb_u_T0u0IuuyIC/page/n215/mode/2up).

[70] On the concept of intention in medieval philosophy, see, e.g., David C. Lindberg, *Theories of Vision from Al-Kindi to Kepler*, p. 259 n. 27: "an intention is that which acts upon and can be grasped by the interior senses or the intellect (as opposed to the five exterior senses)."

ad 5.3 Ad aliud concedo quod si nulla alia propositio fieret nisi ista:
> Verum est,

quod hec foret vera et hoc pro se, et nego consequentiam:
> ergo ista: falsum est, posset consimiliter,

quia quod propositio verificetur pro se, hoc non repugnat significato copule, que significat esse verum, ideo non repugnat copule quod subiectum sic supponat, sed repugnat propositioni non includenti contradictionem quod denotat se esse veram pro se falsa, et ita non sequitur intentum.

E₈ 27ra

ad 5.4 Ad aliud patet per predicta quod non sequitur:
> Iste terminus 'falsum' significat totum cuius est pars,
> ergo supponit pro toto.

Restringitur enim per copulam vel per predicatum respectu cuius supponit, unde non est idem significare et supponere sicut prius probatum est. Et accipitur hic supponere communiter prout est commune ad suppositionem subiecti et ad appellationem predicati. Nec istud videtur mirabile quod iste terminus 'verum' et 'falsum' restringantur per copulam vel predicatum. Videmus enim quod respectu alicuius predicati ampliatur suppositio termini, ut supponat pro hiis que non sunt supposita eius in re, sicut sic dicto:

> Homo erit,
>
> Homo fuit,
>
> Homo est mortuus,
>
> Homo potest esse,

et huiusmodi. Si igitur extrema ex adiunctis copulis vel predicatis talem suppositionem capiunt magis amplam, non videtur mirabile si in aliis possunt termini restringi ne supponant pro omnibus suis significatis. Et hoc patet sic dicendo:

> Homo qui sedet disputat,

non stat hic iste terminus 'homo' pro omni homine. Similiter et modum supponendi multotiens capit subiectum a suo predicato, ut hic:

---

1 aliud] aliam O   3 quod] et O quia E₈   ‖ pro] per O   4 ista] illud O   ‖ consimiliter] similiter O simpliciter E₄   5 quia quod] quorum O   ‖ pro] per O   6 que ... copule] *om.* hom. O   7 includenti] propriam *add.* E₄   8 ita] ideo O   9 aliud] aliam O   10 pars] *om.* E₈   11 toto] tota E₈   12 Restringitur] restringit E₈   ‖ per²] *om.* E₈   13 unde] tamen O   14 Et] *om.* O   15 appellationem] suppositionem O   ‖ istud] id E₄   16 restringantur] restringatur E₄   ‖ vel] per *add.* E₄   17 ampliatur] appropriatur O   18–19 in re, sicut] sicut in re E₈   19 dicto] dicendo O   20 Homo erit] *om.* E₄   21 fuit] homo *add.* E₄   24 et huiusmodi] *om.* E₈   ‖ Si] sic E₈   ‖ extrema] extra E₈   25 videtur] videatur O   ‖ in] eis vel *add.* O   26 ne] ut O   28 sedet] sedens E₄   29 non] nec O   ‖ et] *om.* O   30 predicato] diversum secundum modum a diverso predicato *add. in marg.* E₄

ad 5.3 To the next argument: I grant that if the only proposition were

> A truth exists,

this would be true about itself, and I deny that one can validly infer:

> therefore so too could 'A falsehood exists',

because that a proposition is true about itself is not inconsistent with the signification of the copula, which signifies that the proposition is a truth. So it is not inconsistent with the copula that the subject supposits in this way. But it is inconsistent with a proposition that does not involve a contradiction that it means that it is itself true about its false self. And so what was claimed does not follow.

ad 5.4 To the next argument: it is clear from what has been said that the inference:

> The term 'falsehood' signifies the whole of which it is a part, therefore it supposits for the whole

is invalid. For ⟨its supposition⟩ is restricted by the copula or by the predicate relative to which it supposits. Thus signifying and suppositing are not the same thing, as was proved earlier.[71] And here suppositing is taken broadly insofar as it is common to the supposition of the subject and to the appellation of the predicate. Nor should it be considered strange that the terms 'truth' and 'falsehood' are restricted by the copula or the predicate. For we appreciate that with respect to some predicates a term's supposition is ampliated so that it supposits for things which are not among its presently existing supposita,[72] as in utterances like these:

> A man will exist,
>
> A man existed,
>
> A man is dead,
>
> A man could exist,

and suchlike. Therefore if in this way the extremes receive this broader supposition from the adjoined copulas or predicates, it does not seem strange if in other cases terms can be restricted so that they do not supposit for all their significates. And this is clear in saying, for example:

> The man who is sitting is disputing;

here the term 'man' does not stand for every man. And similarly, the subject often takes the mode of suppositing from its predicate, e.g.,

---

[71] In §4.2.

[72] Ampliation is one of the properties of terms, recognising that some verbs and some terms affect the range of supposition of the subject of the proposition to a broader extension. See, e.g., Read, 'Medieval Theories of Properties of Terms', §4.

Homo est animal,

Homo est species,

aliter supponit subiectum in una quam in alia. Dico igitur quod isti termini 'verum' et 'falsum' et eorum consimilia restringuntur per copulam, que significat esse verum, ut supponant talia pro quibus tota propositio sine contradictione poterit denotare ⟨se⟩ esse veram.

ad 5.5 Ad aliud concedo quod B potest significare totum, sicut dictum est, saltem ⟨per⟩ intentionem universalem, et nego consequentiam:

ergo respectu | cuiuscumque predicati potest supponere totum. E₈ 27rb

Quomodo autem potest significare totum per intentionem singularem et quomodo non, apparebit post.

ad 5.6 Ad aliud, cum dicitur:

"Hic est dici de nullo: 'Nullum falsum dicitur a Sorte'",

concedo; et cum arguitur:

"Nihil est accipere sub subiecto quin ab eo denotatur predicatum removeri",

si illud sic intelligatur:

Nihil est accipere sub subiecto pro quo subiectum supponit quin ab eo denotatur predicatum removeri,

concedo. Et sic intelligit Aristoteles et aliter non.

ad 5.7 Ad aliud concedo quod hec exceptiva est vera:

Nullum falsum preter A dicitur a Sorte,

pro quo sciendum est quod aliqua est exceptiva propria et aliqua impropria. Propria quando fit extra captio partis a suo toto supponente pro illa et intelligitur quod exceptiva repugnat sue preiacenti. Impropria quando

---

1 Homo] hoc E₄   3 supponit subiectum] *inv.* E₄   4 et¹] *om.* O   ǁ et ... copulam] iterum convertibilia restringuntur per copulam E₈ restringuntur per copulam etiam per eorum convertibilia O   5 ut supponant *corr.*] ut supponat E₄ E₈ *om.* O   ǁ pro] de O   ǁ quibus] quo E₄   5–6 propositio ... veram] de quo vel pro quo potest esse verum denominare O   6 poterit] potest E₄   7 aliud] aliam O   ǁ sicut] nunc *add.* E₄   9 cuiuscumque] *om.* O   11 autem] universaliter O   ǁ totum] *om.* O   ǁ intentionem] intellectum O   ǁ et] quantum vel O   13 aliud] aliam et O   14 Hic] hoc E₄   15 concedo] conceditur O   ǁ arguitur] dicitur O   16 accipere] nunc O   ǁ eo] ipso O   19 accipere] capere O   19–20 supponit] supponat O   20 eo denotatur] eodem notatur E₈   21 intelligit] intelligitur O   22 aliud] aliam O   ǁ exceptiva est] *inv.* E₄   24 est¹] *om.* O   25 extra captio] exceptio O   ǁ supponente] supposite *vel* supponente O supposito E₄ supponere E₈

> Man is an animal,
>
> Man is a species;

here the subject supposits differently in the one than in the other. Therefore I say that the terms 'truth' and 'falsehood' and those similar to them are restricted by the copula, which signifies that the proposition is a truth, to supposit for those about which the whole proposition can mean, without contradiction, that it ⟨itself⟩ is true.

ad 5.5 To the next argument: I grant that the expression B can signify the whole, as was said, at least ⟨by means of⟩ the universal intention, and I deny that one can validly infer:

> therefore with respect to any predicate it can supposit for the whole.

And later[73] it will be evident how it can signify the whole by means of a singular intention and how it cannot.

ad 5.6 To the next argument: when it is said:

> "Here we have the *dici de nullo*: 'No falsehood is said by Socrates'"

I grant it; and when it is argued:

> "nothing is taken under the subject without it being meant that the predicate is removed from it",

if this is understood in this way:

> Nothing for which the subject supposits is taken under the subject without it being meant that the predicate is removed from it,

I grant it. And Aristotle understands it in this way and not otherwise.

ad 5.7 To the next argument: I grant that this exceptive is true:

> No falsehood except A is said by Socrates,

about which it should be noted that some exceptives are proper and others are improper.[74] An exceptive is proper when a part is removed from a whole suppositing for that part and it is acknowledged that the exceptive is inconsistent with its prejacent. An exceptive is improper

---

[73] Perhaps a reference to §ad 7.1.1.2.
[74] On proper and improper exceptives, see, e.g., 'Logica Oxoniensis, De Consequentiis', in Pironet, *Guillaume Heytesbury: Sophismata Asinina*, p. 545. A proper exceptive is one where the items excepted constitute a non-empty proper subset of that from which they are excepted; an improper exceptive is one for which they do not.

fit extra captio alicuius quod significatur per illud a quo fit exceptio, licet pro illo non supponat, et sic est in proposito. Aliquando est exceptiva quando neutro modo fit ⟨extra captio⟩, et tunc est improprissima, ut hec:

Nullus asinus preter hominem currit.

ad 5.8.2 Ad aliud concedo quod isti termini convertuntur: 'falsum', et: 'hoc falsum vel illud et sic de singulis', et hoc ut nunc et quoad significata, sed non simpliciter et quoad modum significandi. Et ideo potest unus terminus illorum pro aliquo supponere pro quo non potest alius respectu eiusdem | predicati. Iste enim terminus 'hoc falsum vel illud et sic de singulis', quia significat multa sub disiunctione, scilicet quodlibet illorum significatur singulariter, ideo talis terminus non potest restringi pro uno significato illius | termini in propositione supponere. Et hoc patet in exemplo. Isti termini convertuntur: 'homo' et 'iste homo vel ille et sic de singulis'. Et non sequitur, si iste terminus 'homo', sic dicto:

Homo est species,

posset habere suppositionem simplicem et propositio est vera, quod iste terminus 'iste homo vel ille etc.' posset consimilem habere respectu eiusdem termini, ymmo hoc est simpliciter falsum:

Iste homo vel ille et sic de singulis est species,

vel saltem non admittitur a philosophiis a quibus tamen admittitur alia.

ad 5.9 Ad ultimum dico quod Aristoteles ubi solvit paralogismos secundum accidens docet huiusmodi paralogismos solvere, quia isti peccant secundum eundem defectum, sicut prius probatum est. Variatur enim semper in insolubilibus suppositio termini medii vel extremi; et hoc est facere accidens. Unde tales paralogismi sunt similes insolubilibus ubi medio existente hoc aliquid non coniunguntur extrema. Sic enim arguitur in | insolubilibus, ut:

---

1 extra captio] exceptio O || a quo *corr.*] aliud quod *vel* aliquod quod (*dub.*) E_4 ad quod E_8 aliud pro quo O   2 exceptiva] exceptio E_4 3 hec] hic E_4 dicendo O   5 aliud] aliam O || termini] *om.* E_4 6 et^2] *om.* O || hoc ut] hic et E_8 hoc O || nunc et] *om.* O   7 sed] et E_4 9 eiusdem *corr.*] alterius *mss* || enim] *om.* O   10 singulis] aliis O || scilicet *corr.*] si *mss* 11 singulariter] et *add.* O   11–12 pro uno significato *corr.*] uno significato E_4 E_8 ymmo significatum O   12 propositione] est *add. mss*   13 homo^1] *om.* O || vel] et O   14 homo] potest *add.* O || dicto] dicendo O   16 posset] *om.* O   17 posset *corr.*] possunt E_4 E_8 possint O || consimilem habere] *inv.* O   19 ille] homo *add.* O   20 vel] et E_4 sed O || admittitur^2] admittuntur O   21 ultimum] aliam O || solvit] solvat E_4 22 docet] de *add.* O || paralogismos] sillogismos E_8 paralogismis O   23 enim] *om.* O   24 semper] *om.* E_4 25 Unde] omnes *add.* E_4 || insolubilibus] insolubiles E_4 26 coniunguntur] coniungit O || enim] *om.* O   27 in] *om.* E_4

when something is removed which is signified by that from which the exception is made, although it does not supposit for it. And so it is in the present case. Sometimes a proposition is an exceptive when ⟨the exception⟩ is made in neither of these ways, and then it is most improper, like this:

> No ass except a man runs.

ad 5.8.2 To the next argument: I grant that the terms 'falsehood' and 'this falsehood or that and so on for every instance' are convertible as a matter of fact,[75] and with respect to the significates, but not simply and with respect to the mode of signifying. And thus, one of these terms can supposit for something with respect to the same predicate for which the other cannot. For the term 'this falsehood or that and so on for every instance', since it signifies many things disjunctively (that is, each of these things is signified singularly), for that reason such a term cannot be restricted to supposit for one significate of this term in a proposition. And this is clear in an example. The terms 'man' and 'this man or that and so on for every instance' are convertible. And it does not follow that if the term 'man', in an utterance like this:

> Man is a species

could have simple supposition and the proposition be true, that the term 'this man or that and so on' can have similar supposition with respect to the same term. On the contrary, this:

> This man or that man and so on for every individual is a species,

is unconditionally false and it is not accepted even by those philosophers by whom the other proposition is nonetheless accepted.

ad 5.9 To the final argument: I say that where Aristotle solves paralogisms by the fallacy of accident, he shows how to solve paralogisms of this kind, because they have the same defect, as was proved before.[76] For in insolubles the supposition of the middle or extreme term always varies; and this is to commit the fallacy of accident. Thus these paralogisms are similar to insolubles in which, since the middle term is a this-something, the extremes are not connected. For one argues like this in insolubles, just as here:

---

[75] See Bradwardine, *Insolubilia*, §§6.5.1–2 et alibi.
[76] Chapter 4.

Coriscus cognoscitur a te, Coriscus est veniens, ergo veniens cognoscitur a te,

accipitur enim iste terminus 'veniens', vel saltem intelligi debet cum reduplicatione, et ita variatur suppositio extremi. Et similiter hic:

Omnis triangulus habet tres angulos per se et primo, ysoceles est triangulus, ergo habet tres angulos per se et primo.

Et deficit hic paralogismus sicut in insolubilibus quod medius terminus aliter supponit ⟨in maiori⟩ respectu huius predicati: ⟨habet tres angulos⟩ per se et primo, quam facit in minori, ex qua variatione deficit | a sillogismo. E_8 27vb

Capitulum Sextum
⟨Solutio insolubilium cathegoricorum et ypotheticorum⟩

6.1 Iam restat secundum dictum modum solvere paralogismos ut ⟨dicta⟩ sic applicata magis appareant, et primo de cathegoricis, deinde de ypotheticis.

6.1.1 Ponatur ergo quod sint ⟨tantum⟩ iste tres propositiones:

Deus est,

Homo est,

et

Quodlibet verum est aliquod istorum,

et demonstro illas duas, et hoc dictum proponatur

Quodlibet verum est aliquod istorum.

---

3 enim] autem O || intelligi debet] intelligitur O   4 Et] ita *add.* O   5 Omnis] aliquis O || angulos] et *add.* O || per ... primo] primo et per se O   6 ergo] ysoceles *add.* O   8 hic paralogismus] iste sillogismus O || quod] quia O   10 facit] faciat O || variatione] varietate E_8 O   12 Capitulum Sextum] *rubr. in textu et etiam in marg.* E_8 14 secundum ... solvere] solvere secundum dictum modum O || dictum modum] *inv.* E_4 15 applicata] amplicata E_4 ampliata O || appareant] appareatur E_4 || cathegoricis] cathegoricos E_4 || deinde] secundo O   15–16 de ypotheticis] in ypotheticos E_4 20 et] *om.* E_4 22 duas et *corr.*] deus est E_4 22–23 et ... istorum] *om. hom.* E_8 O

> Coriscus is known by you, Coriscus is approaching, therefore the one who is approaching is known by you,[77]

for the term 'approaching' is taken or at least should be understood re-duplicatively, and so the supposition of the extreme varies.[78] And similarly here:

> Every triangle has three angles by definition, an isosceles is a triangle, therefore it has three angles by definition.[79]

And this paralogism is defective in that, just as in insolubles, ⟨in the major⟩ the middle term supposits differently with respect to the predicate ⟨'has three angles'⟩ by definition than it does in the minor. From this variation ⟨of the middle, this paralogism⟩ is defective as a syllogism.

Chapter 6

⟨Solutions to subject-predicate and compound insolubles⟩

6.1 It now remains to solve paralogisms according to the way described, so that ⟨what has been said⟩ will be clearer when so applied, and applied first to subject-predicate ⟨insolubles⟩, then to compound ones.

6.1.1 So suppose that there are ⟨only⟩ these three propositions:

> God exists,
>
> A man exists

and

> Every truth is one of these,

referring ⟨by 'these'⟩ to the ⟨first⟩ two propositions, and this one is proposed:

> Every truth is one of these.[80]

---

[77] This isn't an insoluble. Segrave is saying that one argues in insolubles in the same way as in the Hidden Man paralogism, that is, as committing the fallacy of accident.

[78] Typical cases of reduplication employ the expressions 'qua' or 'insofar as', e.g., 'I know Coriscus qua the one approaching'. The medievals often used reduplication as a test for whether the fallacy of accident was present. See, e.g., Gelber, 'The Fallacy of Accident and the "dictum de omni"', §IV. So, e.g., Ockham complains that it is commonly said that the Hidden Man paralogism is shown to commit a fallacy of accident since "that he is approaching is distinct from Coriscus insofar as he is known ⟨by you⟩" ([...] dicitur communiter quod hic est fallacia accidentis [...] quia extraneatur Corisco quod sit veniens in quantum cognoscitur): Ockham, *Expositio super libros Elenchorum*, II 9, pp. 231–32.

[79] Cf. Scotus, *Quaestiones super Librum Elenchorum*, Q. 45: "An fallacia accidentis possit causari ex variatione termini', §10 (in *Opera Philosophica*, ed. Andrews et al., vol. II, p. 478), where Scotus has 'figura' in place of 'isosceles'. The question of whether a triangle or an isoceles has three angles by definition alludes to the distinction between two kinds of essential or per se predication: see Aristotle, *Posterior Analytics*, I 4, (73a34 ff.). The first is where the definition of the subject includes the predicate, e.g., species and genus; the second where the definition of the predicate includes the subject, e.g., 'risible' and 'man'.

[80] See Dumbleton, 'Insolubles', §18.2.2 and Brinkley, *Insolubilia*, p. 85 (§160).

Et si negetur, ergo hec est falsa, ergo tantum relique due sunt vere, ergo quodlibet verum est aliquod istorum, quia quelibet est singularis vera. Sed contra: tunc si hec est vera et hoc non est aliquod istorum, ergo aliquod verum non est aliquod istorum, ergo non quodlibet verum est aliquod istorum.

6.1.2 Simile est: ponatur quod tantum iste tres propositiones sint:

> Deus est,
>
> Homo est,

et

> Ista sunt vera omnia

—demonstratis illis duabus, et patet deductio.

6.1.3 Similiter, posito quod tantum iste sint:

> Deus est,
>
> Homo est,

et

> Tantum duo sunt vera,

et patet deductio, quia si sit falsa, tunc duo sunt vera et non plura, ergo tantum duo. Si vera, ergo tria sunt vera, ergo non tantum duo sunt vera.

6.2 Ad solutionem istorum et aliorum, primo videndum est quibus terminis fiat huiusmodi paralogismus. Pro quo est sciendum quod numquam fit iste paralogismus, qui dicitur insolubile, nisi respectu alicuius istorum terminorum: verum, vel: falsum, vel convertibilium suorum—et hoc vel ut nunc [vel hic] vel simpliciter—vel respectu alicuius quod expresse dat intelligere verum vel falsum tamquam partem sui significati, ut: scitum ⟨esse verum⟩, et: scitum esse falsum. Omne enim scitum esse verum est verum, et omne scitum esse falsum est falsum. Tales namque | non possunt supponere pro totis nec convertibilibus nec oppositis nec antecedentibus, ut illos sic supponere foret totum significare se esse falsum vel non esse

E₈ 28ra

---

1 falsa] fallacia O ‖ tantum] unum E₄ ‖ relique due sunt] sunt due relique O   2 est singularis] *inv.* E₈ O   ‖ Sed] si sic E₄   3 si] sic E₄   ‖ hec est] hee essent O   ‖ et hoc non est] *om.* O   4 aliquod¹] alterum O   6 est] istorum *add.* E₄   8–9 est et] *om.* E₄   10 omnia] *om.* O   12 Similiter] simile O   ‖ sint] *om.* O   14 est] *om.* E₄   16 vera] vere O   17 plura] falsa O   18 duo sunt] *inv.* E₄   19 videndum] sciendum E₄   ‖ est] *om.* O in *add.* E₄   20 huiusmodi] iste O   ‖ est] *om.* E₄   21 iste] hic O   ‖ dicitur] est O   22 terminorum] qui dicimus (*dub.*) *add.* O   ‖ et hoc vel] *om.* E₈ O   24 partem] *om.* E₄   ‖ ut] et hoc E₄   24–25 scita ⟨esse verum⟩ et] scitis O   25 Omne enim] esse et O   ‖ esse verum²] *om.* E₄   26 et omne scitum] tunc scitis O   ‖ namque] *om.* O, soli *add.* E₄   28 supponere] suppositis O   ‖ vel] se *add.* O

If you deny it, then it is false, therefore only the other two are true, therefore every truth is one of these because each of them is a true singular proposition. But on the contrary: then if it is true and it is not one of these, therefore some truth is not one of these, therefore it is not the case that every truth is one of these.

6.1.2 It is the same if one supposes that there are only these three propositions:

> God exists,
>
> A man exists,

and

> These are all the truths,

referring ⟨by 'these'⟩ to the ⟨first⟩ two propositions, and the argument is clear.[81]

6.1.3 Similarly, supposing that there are only these propositions:

> God exists,
>
> A man exists,

and

> Only two things are true,

the argument is clear, because if ⟨'Only two things are true'⟩ is false, then two things are true and no more, therefore only two. If ⟨'Only two things are true'⟩ is true, then three things are true, therefore not only two things are true.[82]

6.2 To solve these and other paralogisms, one should first consider which terms give rise to this kind of paralogism. Here it should be realised that the kind of paralogism called insoluble only occurs in relation to one of the terms 'true' or 'false' or what is convertible with them—and this either as a matter of fact or without qualification[83] —or in relation to ⟨an expression⟩ in which we expressly understand 'true' or 'false' as part of its significate, such as 'known ⟨to be true⟩', and 'known to be false'. For everything known to be true is true and everything known to be false is false. In fact such ⟨terms⟩ cannot supposit for wholes nor for convertibles nor for opposites nor for what imply them, as their so suppositing would

---

[81] For those who think that the argument is not so clear after all, they can find it fully developed in Bradwardine, *Insolubilia*, §4.2.7. See also Bradwardine's response, *ibid.* §ad 4.2.7 in ch. 12. See also Dumbleton, 'Insolubles', §18.2.4.
[82] Cf. Bradwardine, *Insolubilia*, §§8.6.3 – ad 8.6.3.1.
[83] For this distinction see §ad 5.8.2 above.

verum. Et quia ista duo solum repugnant significato copule, videlicet verum negari a toto et falsum affirmari de toto, et ideo isti soli termini restringuntur per copulam ne possint supponere pro totis et oppositis et convertibilibus in casu ubi alterum istorum accideret.

ad 6.1.1 Ad primum igitur dico, illo casu posito, quod hec est vera:

> Quodlibet verum est aliquod istorum,

et nego consequentiam:

> Quodlibet verum est aliquod istorum, hoc est verum, ergo hoc est aliquod istorum.

Medium enim variatur, in minori namque supponit pro hoc vero:

> Quodlibet verum est aliquod istorum,

sed in maiori non et ita non sequitur conclusio. Unde sensus maioris est:

> Quodlibet verum aliud ab hoc, vel convertibile cum eo et ita de aliis pro quibus non supponit, est aliquod istorum

et non supponit pro hoc.

ad 6.1.2 Ad aliud:

> Ista sunt omnia vera

⟨est vera⟩. Contra tamen:

> Hec est vera, et hec non est aliqua illorum, ergo illa non sunt omnia vera.

Patet responsio quia iste terminus 'verum' pro alio supponit in maiori quam in conclusione. Sensus enim conclusionis est iste:

> Ista non sunt omnia vera alia ab A,

sit A:

> Ista sunt omnia vera.

Similiter si sic arguatur:

> Ista sunt omnia vera,

demonstratis illis tribus, hec est concedenda. Et tunc arguatur sic:

---

1 Et] *om.* O 3 possint] possent E₄ 5 quod] *om.* O 8 hoc est verum] *iter.* O 10 minori] maiori E₄ 12 in maiori] minori (*dub.*) E₄ 13 eo] hoc E₄ 14 ita] sic O 18 Contra] et *add.* O E₈ 19 Hec] hoc E₄ ‖ hec] *om.* O ‖ illorum] illarum E₄ O 21 alio] aliquo E₄ 23–27 alia ... vera] *om. hom.* E₄ 28 arguatur] arguitur E₄

mean that the whole signified itself to be false or not true. And since only these two possibilities—*viz* 'true' when denied of the whole and 'false' when affirmed of the whole—are inconsistent with the significate of the copula, for that reason these terms alone are restricted by the copula so that they cannot supposit for wholes and opposites and convertibles in a scenario where one of these ⟨inconsistencies⟩ would occur.

ad 6.1.1 Then to the first paralogism I reply that assuming this scenario, this is true:

> Every truth is one of these,

and I deny the validity of the inference:

> Every truth is one of these, this is a truth, therefore this is one of them.

For the middle term varies because in the minor premise it supposits for this truth:

> Every truth is one of these,

but in the major it does not. And so the conclusion does not follow from the premises. For the meaning of the major is:

> Every truth other than ⟨the major premise⟩ (or what is convertible with it and so on for others for which ⟨the subject⟩ does not supposit), is one of these,

and ⟨the subject⟩ does not supposit for ⟨the major premise⟩.

ad 6.1.2 To the next paralogism,

> These are all the truths

⟨is true⟩. To the contrary, however:

> This is a truth, and this is not one of these, therefore these are not all the truths.

The response is clear, because the term 'truth' supposits for something different in the major than in the conclusion.[84] For the meaning of the conclusion is:

> These are not all the truths other than A,

where A is:

> These are all the truths.

Similarly, if one argues like this:

> These are all the truths,

referring to the three propositions, it should be granted.[85] And then if one argues like this:

---

[84] The conclusion is the negation of the insoluble, so subject to the same restrictions.
[85] This is a fourth proposition, like the third, but is true only referring to the first three. It's rather similar to the Revenge Paradox: see, e.g., Bradwardine, *Insolubilia*, 'Introduction', pp. 20–23.

> Ista sunt omnia vera (demonstratis illis tribus), et ista
> sunt omnia vera (demonstratis illis duobus), ergo ista
> tria sunt ista | duo,

ad illud patet quod non sequitur quia variatur medium. Pro pluribus namque supponit in una quam in alia.

ad 6.1.3 Ad tertium patet responsio similiter, quia hec est vera:

> Tantum duo sunt vera,

et non sequitur:

> Hec est vera, ergo non tantum duo sunt vera,

quia ⟨li⟩ 'verum' in antecedente non supponit pro toto nec pro antecedente ad totum suum. Ergo sensus:

> Tantum duo sunt vera, idest tantum duo sunt vera alia
> ab A (sit A totum) vel alia ab antecedentibus ad A etc,

non enim supponit pro A nec antecedentibus ad A.

Sed si arguatur sic:

> Hec tria sunt vera, et alia duo sunt vera, ergo tria sunt
> vera, ergo non tantum duo sunt vera,

negatur prima consequentia, sed sequitur:

> Ergo ista tria sunt vera et ista plura duobus sunt vera,

et non sequitur ultra:

> Ergo tria ⟨sunt vera et plura duobus sunt vera⟩;

sicut non sequitur:

> Hoc dictum a Sorte est falsum, ergo dictum a Sorte est
> falsum,

et causa est quia sic dicto:

> Ista tria sunt vera,

subiectum est terminus singularis et predicatum supponit | pro omnibus demonstratis nec potest restringi.

Sed sic dicto:

28–1 hec ... tribus] *om. hom.* O   4 illud] idem O E₈   ‖ quod non sequitur] solutio O   5 supponit in una] una supponit O   9–11 tantum ... sensus] *om. hom.* O   12 idest] *om.* O   ‖ vera²] *om.* E₄   13 etc] *om.* O   14 nec] pro *add.* O   16 sunt vera¹] est vera E₄ *inv.* O   18 negatur] illa *add.* O   17–19 ergo non ... vera] *om. hom.* E₄   20 ultra] ultimo O   22 sequitur] et *add.* O   23–24 ergo ... falsum] *om. hom.* O   25 dicto] dicendo O   27 predicatum] tria *add.* O   28 demonstratis] *om.* O   29 dicto] dicendo O

> These are all the truths (referring to the three propositions), and these are all the truths (referring to the two propositions), therefore these three are these two,

in response to this it is clear that this inference is not valid because the middle term varies. In fact it supposits for more propositions in one premise than in the other.

ad 6.1.3 Similarly, the response to the third paralogism is clear because this is true:

> Only two things are true,

and the inference

> ⟨'Only two things are true'⟩ is true, therefore not only two things are true

is not valid because 'true' in the premise does not supposit for the whole nor for what implies the whole.[86] So the meaning ⟨of 'Only two things are true' is⟩:

> Only two things are true, that is, only two things are true other than A (where A is the whole, ⟨'Only two things are true'⟩) or other than what implies A, etc.,

for ⟨'true'⟩ does not supposit for A nor for what implies A.

But if one argues like this:

> These three things are true and the other two are true, therefore three things are true, therefore not only two are true,

I deny the first inference, but this follows:

> therefore these three are true and these more than two are true,

and the further conclusion:

> therefore three things ⟨are true and more than two are true⟩

does not follow; just as:

> This utterance of Socrates' is false, therefore an utterance of Socrates' is false

is not valid and the reason is because if one says:

> These three things are true,

the subject is a singular term and the predicate supposits for all the propositions referred to and cannot be restricted.

But if one says:

---

[86] That is, 'true' cannot supposit for 'Two things are true and no more' (see §6.1.3), as stated in §6.2, since it implies 'Only two things are true'.

> Tria sunt vera et plura duobus sunt vera,

li 'verum' non supponit pro A nec antecedentibus ad A, sicut nec facit ⟨in⟩ ista:

> Non tantum duo sunt vera,

hec enim includitur in illa, sed est sensus:

> Plura duobus sunt vera, idest plura duobus sunt vera alia ab hac vel ab antecedentibus ad hanc etc.

6.3.1 Similiter paralogizatur sic: sint tantum hoc:

> Falsum est,

et

> Falsum est hoc,

et sit prima A et demonstretur in secunda A. Tunc aut A est verum vel falsum. Si verum, ergo nihil est falsum, quia nec hoc nec aliud ab hoc, sicut manifeste patet; ergo si falsum | est, nullum falsum est. Si A sit falsum, ergo falsum est hoc, ergo falsum est quia arguitur ab inferiori | ad superius suum.

Simile est de omnibus talibus:

> Nullum tibi propositum est verum,

proponatur tantum illa; et similiter:

> Nullum tibi propositum est concedendum;

et similiter in isto particulari:

> Aliquod propositum tibi non est concedendum.

6.3.2 Simile est: dicat Sortes tantum istam:

> Sortes dicit falsum

et similiter:

> Sortes intelligit falsum,
>
> Sortes credit falsum,
>
> Sortes decipitur,

posito quod: decipi, et: credere falsum, convertantur.

Simile accidit respectu veri negando sic:

---

1 et] vel E$_4$ *om.* O   2 nec^2] non O   3 ista] a E$_4$ 5 hec] hoc E$_4$ hic O   ‖ enim includitur] inducitur O   6 idest ... vera] *om. hom.* E$_8$ 7 ab^2] *om.* E$_4$ E$_8$ 8 sint] si O   9 Falsum est] *inv.* E$_4$ 10 et] *om.* O hoc *add.* E$_4$ 11 est] cum O   12 demonstretur] denominetur E$_4$ E$_8$ ‖ Tunc] queritur *add.* O   ‖ vel] aut O   14 sicut ... patet] si nullum est O   ‖ est^1] *om.* E$_4$ 16 suum] *om.* E$_4$ E$_8$ 21 similiter] simpliciter E$_8$ simile O   22 propositum tibi] *inv.* O   25 similiter] simile O   29 decipi] decipitur E$_4$ ‖ et] *om.* E$_4$ 30 respectu veri] *lacuna in* O   ‖ sic] istam O

> Three things are true and more than two are true,

'true' does not supposit for A nor for what implies A, just as ⟨in⟩ this

> Not only two things are true

⟨'true'⟩ does not ⟨supposit for A nor for what implies A⟩, for ⟨'More than two are true'⟩ implies it, but the meaning ⟨of 'More than two are true'⟩ is

> More than two things are true, that is, more than two things are true other than this one or what implies it etc.

6.3.1 Similarly, a paralogism is made like this: let there be only:

> A falsehood exists,

and

> A falsehood is this,

where the first proposition is A and A is referred to ⟨by 'this'⟩ in the second. Then either A is true or false. If ⟨A⟩ is true, then nothing is false, because neither this nor anything other than this ⟨is false⟩, as is manifestly clear; therefore if a falsehood exists ⟨that is, A is true⟩, no falsehood exists, ⟨therefore A is false⟩. If A is false, then a falsehood is this, therefore a falsehood exists ⟨that is, A is not false⟩, because it is argued from an inferior term to its superior.[87]

It is the same concerning all of these:

> Nothing proposed to you is true,

when only this proposition is proposed; and similarly:

> Nothing proposed to you should be granted;

and similarly in this particular proposition ⟨proposed to you⟩:

> Something proposed to you should not be granted.[88]

6.3.2 It is the same if Socrates says only:

> Socrates says a falsehood,

and similarly:

> Socrates understands a falsehood,
>
> Socrates believes a falsehood,
>
> Socrates is deceived,

supposing that 'to be deceived' and 'to believe a falsehood' are convertible.[89]

The same happens with respect to negating 'truth', like these:

---

[87] As we will see in Segrave's reply (§ad 6.3.1), the inference here is taken not as one "a tertio adiacente ad secundum adiacens" (from a proposition with the copula as third component to one with it as second component), but taking 'hoc' ('this') as inferior to 'ens' ('existing' or 'being').

[88] The allusion here is to *proposita* in an *obligatio*. See 'Introduction', §4.

[89] See Bradwardine, *Insolubilia*, ch. 9.

> Nullum verum est,

posito quod tantum sit ista,

> Nullum verum intelligitur a te,

et ita de consimilibus.

ad 6.3.1 Pro istis: dico ad primam quod hec est falsa:

> Falsum est,

et concedo 'falsum est hoc', et nego consequentiam:

> Hoc est falsum et hoc est, ergo falsum est,

quia iste terminus 'falsum' pro aliquo supponit in maiori pro quo non supponit in conclusione.

Sed arguatur contra hoc:

> Ergo de aliquo dicitur 'hoc' de quo non dicitur 'ens', quod tamen est falsum quia 'hoc' est inferius ad 'ens'.

Ad illud dicitur concedendo quod de aliquo subiecto vere affirmeretur 'ens' et 'hoc', pro aliquo significato eius, de quo subiecto non vere affirmatur antecedens pro illo; et causa est quia illud subiectum non supponit pro illo in tali propositione, sed tamen de illo significato affirmetur 'ens', sic dicto hoc:

> Falsum est ens,

et ita non sequitur quod aliquid sit hoc quod non est ens.

6.3.3 Ad aliam similiter dicitur quod hec est falsa:

> Falsum dicitur a Sorte

et ad deductionem patet.

---

3 te] Sorte O   5 primam] primum E$_8$ 7 est] *om.* E$_4$ E$_8$ 8 est^3] *om.* E$_4$ 9 quia ... falsum] *om.* O || pro aliquo supponit] supponit pro aliquo E$_4$ 9–10 in maiori pro quo non supponit] potest supponere O *om.* E$_4$ 13 tamen] *om.* O   14 illud] aliud O || dicitur] *om.* O || affirmeretur] affirmantur O   15 et] *om.* E$_8$ O || significato eius] *inv.* E$_4$ 17 pro] *om.* E$_4$ || propositione] supponere E$_4$ || tamen] cum E$_8$ O   18 sic dicto] sicut de subiecto O   20 aliquid sit hoc] sit aliquid O || est] sit O   21 aliam ... dicitur] aliud simili contra O

> No truth exists,

supposing that is the only proposition,

> No truth is understood by you,

and so on for similar paralogisms.[90]

ad 6.3.1 With regard to these propositions: I say to the first that this is false:

> A falsehood exists,

and I grant 'A falsehood is this', and I deny the validity of the inference:

> This is a falsehood and this exists ⟨i.e., is a being⟩, therefore a falsehood exists ⟨i.e., is a being⟩,

because the term 'falsehood' supposits for something ⟨sc. A⟩ in the major premise[91] for which it does not supposit in the conclusion ⟨sc. A itself⟩.[92]

But if one may argue against this response:

> Therefore 'this' is said of something of which 'being' is not said, which, however, is false because 'this' is inferior to 'being'.

I reply to this by granting that 'being' and 'this' would be truly affirmed of some subject ⟨sc. 'falsehood'⟩ for one of its significates ⟨sc. A⟩, while the premise is not truly affirmed of that subject for that significate ⟨sc. A⟩; and the reason is that the subject ⟨of A⟩ does not supposit for that significate in that proposition ⟨A⟩, while in an utterance like

> A falsehood is a being

'being' is affirmed for that significate, and thus it does not follow that something is this which is not a being.[93]

6.3.3 To another proposition:

> A falsehood is said by Socrates,

I reply similarly that this is false and the response to the argument is clear.

---

[90] See Bradwardine, *Insolubilia*, §12.2.

[91] The major premise is often taken to be that containing the major term, that is, the predicate of the conclusion. But Segrave seems to be following Peter of Spain and others who define the first premise as the major premise: see Peter of Spain, *Summaries of Logic*, ed. Copenhaver, ch. 4 §2: "Omnis autem sillogismus constat ex tribus terminis et duabus propositionibus. Quarum propositionum prima vocatur maior propositio, secunda minor."

[92] We have expanded the translation in this paragraph to make the argument clearer. Segrave's solution entails that A ('A falsehood exists', equivalently, 'A falsehood is existing' or 'A falsehood is a being') is false and that a falsehood is this, sc. A, even though, or rather because, 'falsehood' in A cannot supposit for A. But from 'A falsehood is this' it seems to follow by an expository syllogism that a falsehood is a being, or exists, contradicting his solution. On the expository syllogism, also known as 'ecthesis', see, e.g., Parsons, 'The Power of Medieval Logic', pp. 192–93 and Buridan, *Treatise on Consequences*, 'Introduction', pp. 21–23.

[93] Recall from Segrave's reply in §ad 5.8.2 that he accepts that for discrete terms, like 'hoc falsum' ('this falsehood'), signification is the same as supposition.

6.3.3.1 Sed si arguatur sic:

> Aliquid dicitur a Sorte et nihil aliud a propositione dicitur
> a Sorte, ergo aliqua propositio dicitur a Sorte,

conceditur quia iste terminus propositio bene potest supponere pro hoc dicto a Sorte, sicut dictum est prius. Et sequitur ultra:

> Propositio dicitur a Sorte, | omnis propositio est vera vel falsa, ergo verum vel falsum dicitur a Sorte.

Et sequitur ultra:

> Verum vel falsum dicitur a Sorte, et non verum, ergo falsum;

iste discursus patet per regulam in disiunctivis.

ad 6.3.3.1 Ad istud: conceditur

> Propositio dicitur a Sorte

et

> Aliquale dicitur a Sorte

et omnia talia; et minorem concedo similiter, sed consequentiam distinguo eo quod potest esse disiunctiva vel de disiuncto extremo. Si disiunctiva, falsa et non sequitur ex premissis. Si de disiuncto extremo, vera est; et sic est unus terminus universalis et communior quam falsum et quam verum simpliciter et potest supponere pro aliquo supposito falsi pro quo non potest iste terminus 'falsum' supponere respectu eiusdem predicati, sicut potest iste terminus 'propositio'. Et sic non sequitur ultra

> Verum vel falsum dicitur a Sorte, et non verum, ergo falsum,

maior enim verificatur pro aliquo pro quo non potest conclusio verificari.

---

1 Sed] *om.* E$_4$ 4 propositio] suppositio O   5–7 Et sequitur ... Sorte] *om. hom.* O
11 iste *corr.*] prius E$_4$ E$_8$ primus O || disiunctivis] discernins E$_4$ dysamis (*dub.*) E$_8$ 12 istud] aliud O || conceditur] concedo quod O   14 et] quod *add.* O   15 Aliquale] aliquid O
16 similiter] simili O   17 disiuncto extremo] disiuncto predicato E$_4$ *inv.* O   19 sic est] si O || terminus] talis O || et^1] *om.* O   20 et] *om.* O || falsi] *dub.* E$_4$ 21 supponere] *post* potest E$_4$ 25 conclusio verificari] *inv.* O

6.3.3.1 But if one argues like this:

> Something is said by Socrates and only a proposition is said by Socrates, so some proposition is said by Socrates,

the inference is granted because the term 'proposition' can rightly supposit for what is said by Socrates, as was said earlier.[94] And further, this is valid:

> A proposition is said by Socrates, every proposition is true or false, therefore a truth or a falsehood is said by Socrates.

And this too is valid:

> A truth or a falsehood is said by Socrates, but not a truth,[95] therefore a falsehood;

this reasoning is clear through the rule of disjunctive syllogism.[96]

ad 6.3.3.1 To this objection, ⟨I respond⟩ by granting

> A proposition is said by Socrates

as well as

> Something true or false is said by Socrates

and all such claims, and I grant the minor premise as well, but I disambiguate the inference insofar as ⟨the conclusion⟩ can be either a disjunction or a proposition with a disjunct extreme.[97] If it is a disjunction, it is false and it does not follow from the premises. If it is a proposition with a disjunct extreme, it is true; and so ⟨its subject⟩ is a universal term and more general than just falsehood or just truth and it can supposit for some suppositum of 'falsehood' for which the term 'falsehood' cannot supposit with respect to the same predicate, as, e.g., the term 'proposition' can. And thus the final inference:

> A truth or a falsehood is said by Socrates, but not a truth, therefore a falsehood,

is not valid, for the major is true of something of which the conclusion cannot be true.

---

[94] See §6.2.

[95] That is, a truth is not said by Socrates.

[96] Literally, "by a rule in disjunctive ⟨propositions⟩". The *Logica Oxoniensis* (the standard logic textbook in Oxford from the mid-fourteenth century) gives two rules for disjunctive propositions: Addition (from one part of an affirmative disjunction to the whole) and Disjunctive Syllogism (from an affirmative disjunction with the denial of one part to the other part). See, e.g., Pironet, *Guillaume Heytesbury: Sophismata Asinina*, p. 563.

[97] That is, the conclusion of the first inference, 'A truth or a falsehood is said by Socrates' can be read either as a disjunctive proposition, 'A truth is said by Socrates or a falsehood is said by Socrates', or as a simple subject-predicate proposition with a disjunct term as subject, 'A truth or falsehood is said by Socrates'. For this distinction, and its importance in the development of the theory of supposition in the fourteenth century, see, e.g., Read, 'Thomas of Cleves and Collective Supposition', esp. §1.

ad 6.3.2 Ad consimilia patet per idem.

6.4 Et similiter ad exclusivas et exceptivas consimili modo est respondendum ut hic:

> Tantum Sortes dicit falsum,

dicat Sortes tantum istam et non loquatur alius; et similiter:

> Nullus homo preter Sortes dicit falsum.

6.5 In disiunctivis et copulativis ut hic:

> Homo est asinus vel disiunctiva tibi proposita est falsa,

et proponatur tibi hec disiunctiva. Si conceditur, ergo secunda pars est falsa et prima similiter, ergo tota disiunctiva. Si negatur, ergo hec est falsa et hec disiunctiva tibi proposita est falsa et hec est secunda pars, ergo secunda pars est vera, ergo disiunctiva est vera.

ad 6.5 Pro istis est sciendum quod disiunctiva, cum hoc quod ipsa sit, significat se esse veram sicut cathegorica, et hoc pro altera parte, unde neganda est ista disiunctiva. Et non sequitur:

> Hec est falsa et hec est disiunctiva tibi proposita, ergo disiunctiva tibi proposita est falsa,

in hac enim

> Disiunctiva tibi proposita est falsa,

que est secunda pars, non | supponit pro ipsa. Sed est sensus: E_8 29ra

> Disiunctiva tibi proposita alia ab hac est falsa

et hec est falsa quia nulla alia tibi proponitur.

6.6 Aliter paralogizatur sic: sit A altera istarum:

> Deus est,

vel

> Nullum propositum Sorti est concedendum a te,

---

1 consimilia] similia O ‖ per] propter E_4 2 exclusivas et exceptivas] exceptivas et exclusivas O   ‖ consimili] simili O   3 ut] *om.* O   4 dicit] dicat E_4 5 loquatur] loquitur E_4 E_8 6 homo ... falsum] dicit falsum preter Sortes O   10 negatur] negetur O ‖ ergo²] *om.* E_8 O   11 et¹] *om.* O ‖ disiunctiva] disiuncta E_8 12 ergo ... vera] *om. hom.* O   13 est sciendum] dicendum O   ‖ quod²] cum E_4 14 significat] significet O   15 Et non sequitur] *om.* O   16 et] *om.* O   ‖ est²] *om.* E_8 O   17 falsa] et hec secunda pars ergo secunda pars est vera *add.* O   19 tibi proposita] *inv.* O   ‖ falsa] falsum E_4 22 alia] *om.* E_8 23 Aliter] alius O   ‖ paralogizatur] paralogismus ponatur O   24 est] *om.* E_4 26 Sorti] *om.* O

ad 6.3.2 The response to similar insolubles, ⟨such as those in 6.3.2,⟩ is clear from that.

6.4 And correspondingly, one should respond to exclusive and exceptive propositions in a similar way, as here:

> Only Socrates says a falsehood,

when Socrates says only that and no one else speaks; and similarly ⟨here⟩:

> No man besides Socrates says a falsehood.

6.5 In disjunctions and conjunctions, such as here:

> A man is an ass or a disjunction proposed to you is false;

let this disjunction be proposed to you. If you grant it, then the second disjunct is false and the first as well, therefore the whole disjunction ⟨is false⟩. If you deny it, then it is false and ⟨so⟩ the disjunction proposed to you is false, and this is the second disjunct, therefore the second disjunct is true, therefore the disjunction is true.

ad 6.5 With regard to these insolubles, it should be recalled that a disjunction, assuming that it exists, signifies itself to be true just as does a subject-predicate proposition, and ⟨to be true⟩ in virtue of one or other disjunct, and for this reason this disjunction should be denied. And the following inference is invalid:

> This is false and this is the disjunction proposed to you,
> therefore a disjunction proposed to you is false,

for in this:

> A disjunction proposed to you is false,

which is the second disjunct,[98] ⟨'false'⟩ does not supposit for the disjunction. But the meaning ⟨of the second disjunct⟩ is:

> A disjunction proposed to you other than this one is false

and this is false because no other disjunction is proposed to you.[99]

6.6 A paralogism can be made in another way like this: let A be one of these:

> God exists,

or

> Nothing proposed to Socrates should be granted by you,

---

[98] That is, the second disjunct of the insoluble in §6.5.
[99] For Segrave's account of conjunctive insolubles, promised in §6.5, see §6.7.

et lateat te, et proponatur Sorti hec:

    A est vera,

et nulla alia; deinde proponatur tibi ista:

    A est verum.

6.6.1 Si ne|ges, contra: sequitur:

    A est 'Deus est', ergo A est verum.

6.6.2 Si dubitetur, contra:

    Quodcumque istorum A significat, A est verum, sed A est alterum istorum, ergo A est verum.

Consequentia patet et minor est vera per positum, maiorem probo quia:

6.6.2.1 si A sit ista

    Deus est,

A est verum.

6.6.2.2 Si sit illa:

    Nullum propositum Sorti est concedendum a te,

A est verum, quia si A sit illa, ex A esse falsum sequitur ipsum esse verum. Sequitur enim:

    A est falsum, ergo 'A est verum' non est concedendum,

et ita nullum propositum sorti est concedendum, quia tantum 'A est vera' proponitur sorti. Et si A sit ista, ergo ex A esse falsum sequitur A esse verum, si A sit hoc

    Nullum propositum sorti et cetera.

6.6.3 Ideo dico ad illud concedendum sicut oportet quod A sit verum.

---

1 te] que *add.* E₄   3 proponatur] proponitur E₄ O || tibi] *om.* E₈ || ista] istam E₈ O   7 contra] *om.* E₄   8 Quodcumque] pro quocumque E₈ O || A²] *om.* E₄ || sed] et O   11 ista] a E₄   16 A¹] *om.* E₄ || ipsum] A O   18 concedendum] ergo *scr. et del.* E₈   19 tantum ... vera *coniecimus*] nullum A *mss*   20 ergo] A est verum ergo *add.* E₈ O   24 Ideo] *om.* O || concedendum] concedo E₄ O quod *add.* O

and let it be unknown to you ⟨which A is⟩; and let

> A is true,

and no other proposition, be proposed to Socrates; then let this be proposed to you:

> A is true.[100]

6.6.1 If you deny ⟨'A is true'⟩, on the contrary, this is valid:

> A is 'God exists', therefore A is true.

6.6.2 If you express doubt about it, on the contrary:

> Whichever of these A signifies, A is true, but A is one of these, so A is true.

The inference is clear and the minor is true by hypothesis. I prove the major because:

6.6.2.1 if A is

> God exists,

A is true.

6.6.2.2 If ⟨A⟩ is:

> Nothing proposed to Socrates should be granted by you,

A is true because if A is that proposition, from A's being false it follows that A is true. For this is valid:

> A is false, therefore 'A is true' should not be granted,

and so nothing proposed to Socrates should be granted, because only 'A is true' is proposed to Socrates. And if A is that, ⟨that is,⟩ if A is:

> Nothing proposed to Socrates ⟨should be granted by you⟩,

from A's being false it follows that A is true.

6.6.3 Hence I say that ⟨the insoluble⟩ should be granted, as it is necessary that ⟨either way, whichever proposition A is,⟩ A is true.[101]

---

[100] This paralogism is essentially the same as a slightly simpler one in Bradwardine, *Insolubilia*, §9.5.3, where 'Nothing proposed to Socrates should be granted by you' is replaced by 'Nothing proposed should be granted by you', since in Segrave's case what is proposed to Socrates ('A is true'—'A est vera') and to you ('A is true, or a truth'—'A est verum') are equivalent. Bradwardine helpfully labels 'God exists' B, 'Nothing proposed should be granted by you' C and 'A is a truth' D. Segrave will later (§6.6.3.2) label 'Nothing proposed to Socrates should be granted by you' B.

[101] This is Segrave's verdict on the insoluble: 'A is a truth' can't be denied (by the argument in §6.6.1) and it can't be doubted (by the argument in §6.6.2) so 'A is a truth' must be granted. Nonetheless, as we will see, A itself must be doubted.

6.6.3.1 Sed arguatur sic: hoc est verum (demonstrando hoc 'A est verum'), et hoc est propositum sorti, ergo aliquod propositum sorti est concedendum a te, ergo hec est falsa:

Nullum propositum sorti est concedendum a te,

et tu dubitas an sit ista, ergo male concessisti.

ad 6.6.3.1 Ad illud respondeo et dubito hanc consequentiam:

Hoc est concedendum a te, et hoc est propositum sorti, ergo aliquod propositum sorti est concedendum a te,

quia si A sit:

Deus est,

consequentia est bona. Si A sit alia, non valet propter causas predictas.

6.6.3.1.1 Sed arguatur contra hoc sic: concessa hac

A est verum,

proponitur | hec: E_8 29rb

Nullum propositum Sorti est concedendum a te,

hec est dubitanda, ut patet, sit illa B, et arguatur sic:

B est tibi dubium, et A est B, ergo A est tibi dubium.

Consequentia est bona et antecedens est tibi dubium, ergo consequens non est a te negandum, sed consequens est falsum quia: A est verum, est scitum a te.

---

1 arguatur] arguitur O   3–4 ergo ... a te] *om. hom.* E_8 O   5 ista] ita O   ‖ male *coniecimus*] multa *mss*   6 respondeo] respondetur E_8 11 predictas] prius dictas E_4 9–15 quia ... te] *om. hom.* O   16 arguatur] arguitur O

6.6.3.1 But one may argue like this: this is true (referring to 'A is true') and this is proposed to Socrates, therefore something proposed to Socrates should be granted by you, therefore

> Nothing proposed to Socrates should be granted by you

is false, and you are in doubt whether ⟨A⟩ is this, therefore you have granted it badly.

ad 6.6.3.1 In response to this, I express doubt about this inference:

> This should be granted by you and this is proposed to Socrates, therefore something proposed to Socrates should be granted by you,

because if A is:

> God exists

the inference is valid. ⟨But⟩ if A is the other proposition, the inference is invalid for the reasons expressed before.[102]

6.6.3.1.1 But one may argue to the contrary like this: having granted

> A is true,

this is proposed:

> Nothing proposed to Socrates should be granted by you.

call it B. This should be doubted, as is clear.[103] And one may argue like this:

> B is uncertain for you and A is B, therefore A is uncertain for you.[104]

The inference is valid and the ⟨minor⟩ premise is uncertain for you, therefore the conclusion should not be denied by you;[105] but the conclusion is false because 'A is true' is known by you.

---

[102] Note that if A is 'Nothing proposed to Socrates should be granted by you', the conclusion of the inference is the contradictory of A and so by Segrave's lights, 'proposed to Socrates' cannot supposit for 'A is true', and accordingly the conclusion is false since its subject is empty. But in the minor premise, 'proposed to Socrates' does supposit for 'A is true'. Hence, in that case, the inference is invalid and commits a fallacy of accident by the variation of supposition of the minor term.

[103] We have seen that Segrave cannot grant the conclusion of the inference in §ad 6.6.3.1 or its contradictory. So although he grants 'A is true', he doubts A, if A is B.

[104] 'dubium' means not knowing either way, connoting ignorance rather than doubt. So we have rendered 'dubium' as "to be uncertain", in line with its role in obligations treatises (see, e.g., Paul of Venice, *Logica Magna: Tractatus de scire et dubitare*, tr. Clarke, pp. xix–xx and Paul of Venice, *Logica Magna: Tractatus de obligationibus*, ed. and tr. Ashworth, p. xv), although we have kept 'express doubt' for 'dubitare'.

[105] An example of Kilvington's notorious disputational meta-argument: see Richard Kilvington, *Sophismata*, sophisms 45–48 *passim*, and Kretzmann's commentary, pp. 316, 324.

ad 6.6.3.1.1 Ad istud respondetur concedendo ultimam consequentiam et dubitando antecedens et consequens; bene ista stant simul:

'A est verum' est scitum a me,

et

A est mihi dubium,

quia si A sit illa

Deus est,

A non est mihi dubium. Si A sit B, tunc est mihi dubium A; et quia nescio utrum A sit

Deus est,

vel alia, nescio utrum sit mihi dubia vel non.

6.7 Eodem modo respondendum est ad copulativas cuiusmodi sunt iste:

Deus est et nulla copulativa tibi proposita est vera,

et hec:

Homo est asinus et copulativa tibi proposita est a te neganda,

et ad omnia similia est eodem modo respondendum.

6.8 Ut autem facilius respondere sciatur ad insolubile propositum, sciendum quod in propositione affirmativa ubi subicitur iste terminus 'verum' respectu termini transcendentis vel cuiuscumque predicati superioris ad verum vel respectu convertibilis numquam accidit insolubile, sed potest pars supponere pro toto et totum verificari pro se, et omnis talis est concedenda:

Omne verum est ens,

Verum est propositio,

Verum est aliquale,

Verum est verum,

et similia. | In affirmativa vero ubi subicitur predicato inferiori ad ipsum bene potest accidere insolubile et quod pars non supponat pro toto cuius est pars, ut hic:

E₄ 161ra

---

1 respondetur] respondetur E₄ respondeo O ‖ ultimam] *om.* E₈ O   2 bene] sive (*dub.*) E₄ unde(*dub.*) O   5 A] *om.* O   8 sit] est E₄ ‖ A; et] *om.* O   9 A sit] *om.* E₄ E₈   11 alia] aliud O ‖ sit mihi] *inv.* E₄   12 est] *om.* E₄ ‖ cuiusmodi] ut O   13 copulativa] est *add.* O ‖ vera] una E₄   15 proposita] a me *add.* O   17 similia] alia E₈ ‖ est eodem modo] eodem modo est E₄ ‖ respondendum] *om.* O   18 respondere sciatur] *inv.* E₈ O ‖ propositum] proponenda O   18–19 sciendum] est *add.* O   19 subicitur] est subiectum O   20 vel] *om.* O   22 et omnis] *om.* O   27 Verum est verum] *om.* O   28 In] nam O ‖ vero] vera O ‖ subicitur] subiecto O   30 pars] *om.* E₄ E₈

ad 6.6.3.1.1 I respond to this by granting the last inference[106] and expressing doubt about the premise and the conclusion; these can stand together

> 'A is true' is known by me,

and

> A is uncertain for me,

because if A is

> God exists,

A is not uncertain for me, ⟨while⟩ if A is B, then A is uncertain for me. And because I do not know whether A is

> God exists

or the other proposition, I do not know if it is uncertain for me or not.

6.7 One should respond in the same way to conjunctions like these:[107]

> God exists and no conjunction proposed to you is true,

and

> A man is an ass and a conjunction proposed to you should be denied by you,

and one should respond in the same way to all similar insolubles.

6.8 To know how to respond more easily to a proposed insoluble, note that in ⟨the case of⟩ an affirmative proposition whose subject is the term 'truth' with respect to a transcendental term or any predicate superior to ⟨the term⟩ 'truth' or with respect to a convertible term, an insoluble never results, but the part can supposit for the whole and the whole can be truly said of itself;[108] and all such propositions should be granted:

> Every truth is a being,
>
> A truth is a proposition,
>
> A truth is true or false,
>
> A truth is true,

and the like. However, in ⟨the case of⟩ an affirmative proposition where ⟨the term 'truth'⟩ is the subject of a predicate inferior to ⟨the term 'truth'⟩ an insoluble can readily result, and ⟨then⟩ the part does not supposit for the whole of which it is part, as here:

---

[106] That is, that the conclusion is false because 'A is true' is known by you.
[107] This paragraph is perhaps misplaced, and should follow §ad 6.5.
[108] See Paul of Venice, *Logica Magna, Tractatus de terminis*, ed. and tr. Kretzmann, p. 291, note *p* to p. 13: "A transcendental term is a simple term (e.g. 'Being') that can be the predicate term in a true affirmative proposition about absolutely anything there is [...] Each transcendental term can therefore be the predicate term in a true affirmative proposition in which any other transcendental term is the subject term."

> Quodlibet | verum est aliquod istorum,
>
> Quodlibet verum est A vel B,
>
> Quodlibet verum est: Deus est.

In talibus enim non potest totum denotare se esse verum pro se et ideo pars non supponit totum in talibus propositionibus, sed sunt tales propositiones concedende pro aliis ab illis propositionibus. Sed e contra est in negativis ubi subicitur iste terminus 'verum' predicato superiori vel convertibili: numquam supponit pars totum sed tantum pro aliis a toto, ut hic:

> Nullum verum est,
>
> Nullum verum est verum,

et similia. Est enim sensus:

> Nullum verum est aliud ab hoc vel convertibili vel antecedente ad hoc,

et similiter respectu predicati inferioris ut hic:

> Nullum verum est aliquod istorum

est sensus:

> Nullum verum aliud ab hoc etcetera est aliquod istorum,

unde pro eisdem supponit terminus in affirmativa et in sui contraria.

6.8.1 Sed iste terminus 'falsum' respectu predicati transcendentis vel cuiuscumque superioris vel convertibilis vel etiam inferioris numquam supponit pro toto in affirmativa.

Et quelibet talis est neganda, si non sit alia ab ista, ut sic dicto:

> Falsum est,
>
> Falsum dicitur a Sorte;

respectu tamen predicati inferioris est concedenda in casu ut hic:

> Quodlibet falsum est aliquod istorum,

demonstratis

> Homo est asinus

et

> Deus non est,

---

1 istorum] et *add.* O 3 verum] talem E$_8$ ‖ Deus est] deus E$_8$ de se intelligibile O 4 non] nec E$_4$ ‖ totum denotare se] denotare se totum E$_4$ ‖ pro] per O 5 totum] pro toto O ‖ propositionibus] *om.* E$_4$ E$_8$ ‖ sunt tales] sicut E$_4$ 6 concedende] accipiende O sunt *add.* E$_4$ 8 totum] vel pro suo toto *add.* O 10 est] verum *add.* E$_8$ 11 Nullum] *om.* E$_8$ O ‖ verum^2] *om.* O 13 est] *post* ad hoc E$_4$ ‖ aliud] a E$_4$ 15 hic] *om.* E$_4$ 16 Nullum] nullus E$_4$ 17 est sensus] *inv.* O 18 aliud] *om.* E$_8$ ‖ etcetera] *om.* O 19 eisdem] eadem E$_4$ ‖ sui] sua O 20 vel] ut O 21 convertibilis] eius *add.* O ‖ etiam] eius O 23 dicto] dicendo O 27 falsum] verum O 28 demonstratis] istis *add.* O

> Every truth is one of these,
> Every truth is A or B,
> Every truth is 'God exists'.

For in such propositions the whole cannot mean that it is true of itself and so the part does not supposit for the whole in such propositions, but they should be granted as speaking of propositions other than these. But on the other hand, in negative propositions in which the term 'truth' is the subject of a superior or convertible predicate: the part never supposits for the whole, but only for things other than the whole, as here:

> No truth exists,
> No truth is true,

and the like. For the meaning is:

> No truth exists other than this or one convertible with or implying it;

and it is the same with respect to an inferior predicate, as here:

> No truth is any of these,

the meaning is:

> No truth other than this ⟨or one convertible with or implying it⟩ is any of these,

because a term supposits for the same things in an affirmative proposition and in its contrary.

6.8.1 But the term 'falsehood' ⟨as subject⟩ with respect to a transcendental or any superior or convertible or even inferior predicate never supposits for the whole in an affirmative proposition.

And if there is no proposition other than this one, every proposition like the utterances:

> A falsehood exists,
> A falsehood is said by Socrates,

should be denied. However, ⟨an affirmative proposition where the term 'falsehood' is the subject⟩ with respect to an inferior predicate should be granted in a scenario like this:

> Every falsehood is one of these,

referring to

> A man is an ass,

and

> God does not exist;

et in tali casu numquam accidit insolubile.

Similiter et in negativa iste terminus 'falsum' non supponit pro toto ut hic:

> Nullum falsum est,
>
> Nullum falsum est propositio,

unde bene iste terminus 'falsum' numquam supponit totum cuius est pars nec in affirmativa nec in negativa, sed est sensus semper | talis: E_8 29vb

> Falsum est, idest falsum aliud ab hoc est,

similiter

> Nullum falsum est, idest nullum falsum aliud ab hoc.

Et iste regule intelligende sunt in propositionibus non includentibus contradictionem ex repugnantia terminorum.

6.9 Sed contra ista arguitur quod iste terminus 'verum' numquam supponit | pro toto sicut nec iste terminus 'falsum', et hoc sic quia si ista propositio: O 2ra

> Verum est

posset verificari pro se vera, cum illud pro quo verificatur propositio sit causa veritatis propositionis et prius naturaliter ⟨quam veritas eius⟩, sequitur quod istam propositionem esse veram foret causa sue veritatis. Consequens est falsum. Et istam positionem ponunt illi quare in insolubilibus non supponit pars pro toto nec convertibili etc.

ad 6.9 Ad illud dico quod illud pro quo verificatur propositio non semper est causa veritatis propositionis nec prius naturaliter quam veritas eius. Hoc patet, nam hec est vera:

> Chymera non est

per non esse chymere. Non esse tamen chymere nihil ponit, ergo nullius positivi est causa. Et similiter de aliis negativis; privatio enim vel non

---

1 et] *om.* E_8 O || insolubile] *om.* E_8 O   2 et] *om.* O || toto] tota E_8 4 Nullum] verum E_8 O || est propositio] proponitur O   6 pars] *om.* E_4 E_8 || affirmativa ... negativa] negativa nec in affirmativa E_4 7 idest] illud E_4 esse *add.* E_8 10 intelligende] intendende E_4 || includentibus] concludentibus E_4 12 arguitur] scilicet *add.* E_8 sic O   12–13 supponit] supponitur E_4 13 toto] tota E_8 17 et] *om.* O   18 quod] *om.* O || esse] fore O || foret] esset O   19 est falsum] ergo etiam antecedens *add.* O || quare] quia O   22 propositionis] ut prius *add.* O || naturaliter] est *add.* O   25 nullius] illius E_4 26 vel] et O

and in such a scenario an insoluble never results.

Similarly, even in a negative proposition the term 'falsehood' does not supposit for the whole, as here:

> No falsehood exists,
>
> No falsehood is a proposition,[109]

for the term 'falsehood' never properly supposits for the whole of which it is part either in an affirmative or in a negative proposition, and the meaning is always:

> A falsehood exists, that is, a falsehood other than this one exists,

similarly

> No falsehood exists, that is, no falsehood other than this one.

And these rules ⟨that is, in §§6.8 and 6.8.1⟩ should be understood concerning propositions not implying a contradiction arising from the incompatibility of the terms.

6.9 But one can argue against these claims that the term 'truth' never supposits for the whole just like the term 'falsehood', and this is so because if the proposition

> A truth exists,

could be true about its true self—since that about which a proposition is true is the cause of truth of the proposition and naturally prior ⟨to its truth⟩[110]—it follows that this proposition's being true would be the cause of its truth. The conclusion is false. And those who make this claim[111] do so on the ground that in insolubles the part does not supposit for the whole nor for what is convertible etc.

ad 6.9 I reply to this objection that that about which a proposition is true is not always the cause of truth of the proposition nor is it naturally prior to its truth. This is clear since the proposition:

> A chimera does not exist

is true on account of the chimera's non-being. However, the chimera's non-being does not posit anything, therefore it is the cause of nothing

---

[109] See §4.1.1. Just as there, the actual insoluble proposition is not spelled out by Segrave. These two propositions do not seem to be insolubles themselves, but are the contradictory of the insolubles 'A falsehood exists' and 'A falsehood is a proposition'. So just as in §4.1.1, we can present a problematic argument which is solved by Segrave's principle that neither 'truth' nor 'falsehood' can supposit for the opposite of the whole proposition of which it is part any more than for the proposition itself.
[110] Added in light of the reply in §ad 6.9.
[111] This claim can be found in the *Tractatus Sorbonniensis Alter*: see Pozzi, *Il Mentitore e il Medioevo*, p. 57 (and pp. 76 and 82, §§1.043 and 1.0721).

esse non est causa alicuius rei positive. Et similiter in propositionibus falsis, hec:

Homo est asinus

falsa est pro eo quod non est ita sicut significat, sed non esse ita sicut significat nihil ponit, ergo non est causa alicuius.

Et similiter veritas huius:

Antichristus erit,

non presupponit illud pro quo verificatur tamquam prius naturaliter ⟨quam veritas eius⟩. Causa ergo veritatis propositionis non semper est illud | pro quo verificatur nisi causa sine qua non sit. Ideo est propositio vera quia significat esse quod est vel non esse quod non est; et ideo falsa est quia significat esse quod non est vel non esse quod est. Et ideo sumitur illud pro quo verificatur propositio sicut prius sive posterius sive simul natura cum veritate propositionis. Deinde propositio significat esse quod est et solum illud, vel non esse quod non est. Hoc sufficit ad veritatem propositionis.

Similiter secundum istum modum dicendi, ut videtur, non potest dari causa quare pars non potest supponere pro antecedente ad totum, cum antecedens ad totum sit causa et prius naturaliter multotiens suo consequente. Similter convertibile cum toto multotiens est prius tempore et secundum istum modum dicendi nihil obstaret quin pro eo fieret suppositio in suo convertibili. Consequens falsum quia utroque modo multotiens accidit insolubile.

E_8 30ra

6.10 In aliis casibus verum vel falsum tamquam partem sui significati paralogizatur sic: proponatur hec:

Aliquod tibi propositum est nescitum a te,

que sit A, et queratur aut A est verum vel falsum. Si verum, et tantum A est propositum, ergo nullum tibi propositum est nescitum a te, quia

---

4 est^2] om. E_4 ‖ ita^1] om. O   4–5 sed non ... significat] igitur respondendo (dub.) E_4 4 esse corr.] est mss   5 ponit] et add. O   6 Et] om. O ‖ huius] huiusmodi E_4 7–8 erit non] non est E_8 O   10 causa] om. E_4 ‖ sit] om. E_8 O   11 significat] ita add. O ‖ quod^1] sicut O   12 est^1] om. E_4 E_8 ‖ significat] non add. O ‖ non^1] om. O ‖ vel] et E_8 O ‖ non^2] om. O ‖ quod^2] non add. O ‖ sumitur] sumuntur O   15 est^2] et add. O   16–17 propositionis similiter] inv. E_4 17 ut videtur] om. O ‖ potest] posset O   18 potest] om. E_4 19–20 suo consequente] subiecto consequentis O   21 dicendi] ponendi E_4 E_8 ‖ quin] quando E_4 E_8 ‖ fieret] sic esset E_8 sic O   22 in] et O ‖ Consequens] est add. O   23 accidit] est O   24 casibus corr.] conclusionibus mss ‖ partem] parte O ‖ significati] om. O   25 paralogizatur] post falsum O ‖ sic] sicut O   27 et^1] tunc O ‖ verum vel falsum] falsum vel verum O   27–28 tantum A est] tantum E_4 tamen E_8

positive. And it is the same concerning other negative propositions, for privation or non-being is not the cause of any positive thing. And it is the same in false propositions; this proposition:

> A man is an ass

is false because things are not as it signifies; but things not being as the proposition signifies does not posit anything, therefore it is not the cause of anything ⟨positive⟩.

And similarly, the truth of

> The Antichrist will exist,

does not require that about which it is true to be naturally prior ⟨to its truth⟩. Therefore the cause of the truth of a proposition is not always that about which it is true unless it is the cause *sine qua non*. For that reason, a proposition is true because it signifies that what is, is or that what is not, is not; and for the ⟨same⟩ reason, a proposition is false because it signifies that what is not, is or that what is, is not.[112] And for the same reason, that about which a proposition is true is supposed to be naturally either prior to or posterior to or simultaneous with the proposition's truth. Then, a proposition signifies that what is, is and only that, or that what is not, is not. This suffices for the truth of a proposition.

Similarly, according to this way of speaking ⟨in terms of causes⟩ it is not possible, as we have seen, that a cause be given why a part cannot supposit for what implies the whole, since what implies the whole is a cause ⟨of the whole⟩ and often naturally prior to what it implies. Similarly what is convertible with the whole is often temporally prior to it and according to this way of speaking ⟨in terms of causes⟩ nothing would stand in the way of its suppositing for it in what is convertible with it. The conclusion ⟨that nothing would stand in the way ...⟩ is false because an insoluble often results in both ways, ⟨temporal and natural⟩.

6.10 In other cases, a paralogism can be made with truth or falsehood as part of its significate like this: let this be proposed to you:

> Something proposed to you is unknown by you,[113]

call it A, and ask if A is true or false. If ⟨you reply that A is⟩ true, and only A is proposed to you, then nothing proposed to you is unknown by

---

[112] A paraphrase of Aristotle's famous definition of truth and falsehood at *Metaphysics*, Γ 7, 1011b25–27: "dicere namque ens non esse aut hoc esse, falsum, ens autem esse et non ens non esse, verum est".
[113] Cf. Pozzi, *Il Mentitore e il Medioevo*, p. 340 example (35): "aliquod tibi propositum nescitur a te".

tu scis A esse verum. Si negatur A, contra tunc sic: tu scis A esse falsum, et A est tibi propositum, ergo tibi propositum est nescitum a te, ergo A est verum. Si dubitatur, ergo A est non scitum, ergo est nescitum, ergo aliquod propositum est nescitum a te.

ad 6.10 Pro quo sciendum est quod aliud est nescire quam non scire sicut aliud est nolle quam non velle. Non scire enim | nihil ponit sed nescire ponit actum scire contrarium. Unde nescire proprie est cognoscere aliquod esse falsum vel errare circa verum. E_8 30rb

Hoc posito hec est neganda:

    Aliquod tibi propositum est nescitum a te,

quia est sensus iste:

    Aliquod tibi propositum est scitum a te esse falsum,

et patet quod extrema propositionis non supponunt pro toto, sicut nec in ista:

    Propositum tibi est falsum.

Et ita non sequitur:

    A tibi propositum est nescitum a te, ergo aliquod tibi
    propositum est nescitum a te,

quia extrema in conclusione non supponunt pro A pro quo supponunt in antecedente.

6.10.1 Alia opinio que ponit partem supponere pro toto aliter responderet ad huiusmodi sophysmata. Concedit namque hec positio quod A est falsum, et cum arguitur:

    A est nescitum a te, et A est tibi propositum, ergo ⟨ali-
    quod⟩ tibi propositum est nescitum a te,

concedit conclusionem, sed dicit quod hec non est A, sed similis ei.

ad 6.10.1 Sed hec responsio faciliter improbatur quia ponendo quod subiectum ipsius A supponit pro A, tunc A non significat nisi A nescitur a

---

1 scis^1] sis E_4 || negatur] negetur O || A^2] om. E_8 || contra tunc] tunc O om. E_4 || scis^2] sis E_4 2 et] om. E_4 || a te] om. E_4 E_8 3 dubitatur] dubitetur E_8 O || est ... ergo] om. O 4 a te] om. E_4 E_8 5 sciendum est] inv. O || nescire ... scire] non scire quam nescire O 6 nolle ... velle] non velle quam nolle O || enim] om. O || nihil] non E_4 || sed] om. O || nescire] aut add. O 7 scire contrarium] inv. E_4 || aliquod] aliquid O 10 tibi propositum] inv. E_4 11 est sensus] inv. E_4 12 tibi] om. E_8 13 quod] quia E_8 O 17 nescitum a te] a te nescitum O 19 conclusione] propositione O || pro A] om. O || supponunt^2] supponit E_8 21 partem] parte E_4 || pro toto] om. E_4 22 huiusmodi sophysmata] hoc sophysma O || hec positio quod] depositio quia O 23 cum] tamen E_4 est tunc O 24 nescitum] negatum E_4 25 nescitum] negatum E_4 26 sed^1] et O || hec] hoc O || ei] a O 27 responsio] sic add. E_4 || ponendo] in posito O 28 supponit] supponat O

you, because you know that A is true. If you deny A, then I argue to the contrary like this: you know that A is false, and A is proposed to you, therefore something proposed to you is unknown by you, therefore A is true. If you express doubt ⟨about A⟩, then A is not known, therefore it is unknown, therefore something proposed to you is unknown by you.

ad 6.10 Here it should be realised that to be unknown is not the same as not to know, just as to be unwilling is not the same as not to be willing. For not to know does not affirm anything, while to be unknown affirms an act contrary to knowing.[114] Thus, properly, to be unknown is to know that something is false or to be mistaken about the truth.[115]

Having stated that, this should be denied:

>Something proposed to you is unknown by you,

because the meaning is

>Something proposed to you is known by you to be false,

and it is clear that the extremes of the proposition do not supposit for the whole, just as they ⟨do not supposit for the whole⟩ in

>What is proposed to you is false.

And so the inference:

>A, which is proposed to you, is unknown by you, therefore something proposed to you is unknown by you,

is not valid because the extremes in the conclusion do not supposit for A, for which they do supposit in the premise.

6.10.1 Another opinion, which claims that a part can supposit for the whole, would respond differently to sophisms of this kind. For this solution grants that A is false, and when it is argued:

>A is unknown by you and A is proposed to you, therefore ⟨something⟩ proposed to you is unknown by you,

it grants the conclusion but says that it is not A, but a proposition similar to it.[116]

ad 6.10.1 But this response can be easily disproved because, assuming that A's subject supposits for A, then A signifies only that A is unknown

---

[114] That is, *non scire/velle* is a negatio negans, *nescire/nolle* a negatio privans. See, e.g., Ashworth, *Logic and Language in the Post-Medieval Period*, p. 190.
[115] Even if what is said here is true of the Latin verb 'nescire' and adjective 'nescitum', it is not true of the English adjective 'unknown'. According to Segrave, 'nescire' means "to know not to be the case", and there seems to be no verb or adjective in English corresponding exactly to this. So faute de mieux we continue to use 'unknown' (since Segrave clearly equates 'nescire' with 'esse nescitum'), but the reader should bear this always in mind.
[116] See Bradwardine, *Insolubilia*, §ad 9.2.

te, et hoc est verum secundum istam positionem, ergo A significat verum et solum verum, ergo A est verum. Assumptum patet quia subiectum A non supponit nisi pro A, ergo tantum denotat predicatum sibi inesse, et hoc est verum, ergo etc. Et ita patet insufficientia istius responsionis.

6.11 Aliter paralogizatur sic: proponatur ista:

>Aliquod tibi propositum non est scitum a te,

vel ista

>Nullum tibi propositum est scitum a te,

que sit A. Et queratur | de A: aut sit vera aut falsa, et patet deductio.

ad 6.11 Ad illud respondeo concedendo A, et cum arguitur:

>A scitur | a te, et A est tibi propositum, ergo aliquid tibi propositum scitur a te,

dico quod consequentia hec non valet. Non enim potest subiectum huius:

>Aliquod tibi propositum est scitum a te,

supponere pro A, que est eius contradictoria, quia hoc foret significare seipsam esse falsam. Et ita patet quod nec in A subiectum supponat nec in eius contradictorio quia in contradictoriis termini pro eodem supponunt.

6.12 Aliter paralogizatur sic: proponatur hec:

>Hoc tibi propositum est tibi dubium,

que sit A, et queratur aut A sit verum vel falsum. Si concedatur, aliquod tibi propositum est tibi dubium, contra: | nec A est tibi dubium nec aliquod aliud propositum ab A, ergo nullum propositum est tibi dubium. Si dubitetur A, contra: A est tibi dubium, et A est tibi propositum, ergo propositum est tibi dubium. Similiter patet quod non potest dubitari quia nec pro alio nec pro se. Pro alio non est A dubitanda quia constat quod nihil aliud ab A est tibi propositum; nec est dubitanda pro se ipsa quia si subiectum supponat pro toto, hec consequentia est bona:

---

1 A] om. O   4 hoc] hec E₈ || est verum] om. E₄   5 sic] et add. O || ista] om. O   6 scitum] nescitum O   7 ista] illud O   9 que] om. E₄ || queratur] queritur E₈ || sit²] est O || aut²] est add. O   10 respondeo] responditur O || concedendo] maiorem add. O   12 scitur] est scitum O   13 consequentia hec] conclusio illa O || Non] nec O || huius] scilicet add. O   15–17 contradictoria ... eius] om. hom. O   15 quia] quod E₈   16 supponat] supponit E₄   17 eodem] eisdem E₈   18 proponatur] proponitur E₈ ponatur O   19 Hoc] om. E₄   20 vel] aut O   21 A est] inv. E₄   22 aliud] om. E₄ E₈ || propositum²] tibi add. O || est tibi] inv. O   23–24 si ... dubium] om. hom. O   24 Similiter patet] simile vel simul (dub.) potest E₄   24–25 quia ... nec] om. O   25–26 Pro alio non... pro se] om. hom. O   26 ipsa] ipso O   27 supponat] supponit O || toto] tota O

by you, and this is true[117] according to this solution, therefore A signifies a truth and only a truth, therefore A is true. The assumption is clear because A's subject does not supposit except for A, therefore it means only that the predicate inheres in ⟨A⟩ itself, and this is true,[118] therefore ⟨A is true⟩. And so the inadequacy of this response is clear.

6.11 A paralogism can be made in another way like this: let this:

> Something proposed to you is not known by you,

or

> Nothing proposed to you is known by you,

be proposed, call it A, and ask about A if it is true or false, and the argument is clear.[119]

ad 6.11 To this I respond by granting A and when it is argued:

> A is known by you and A is proposed to you, therefore something proposed to you is known by you,[120]

I reply that this inference is not valid. For the subject of

> Something proposed to you is known by you

cannot supposit for A, which is its contradictory, because it would make it signify that it itself is false. And so it is clear that neither in A nor in its contradictory does the subject supposit ⟨for A⟩, because in contradictories the terms supposit for the same thing.

6.12 A paralogism can be made in another way like this: let this:

> This, which is proposed to you, is uncertain for you,

be proposed, call it A, and ask if A is true or false. If you grant it, something proposed to you is uncertain for you—on the contrary: neither A nor anything proposed other than A is uncertain for you, therefore nothing proposed is uncertain for you. If you express doubt about A—on the contrary: A is uncertain for you and A is proposed to you, therefore what is proposed is uncertain for you. Similarly it is clear that ⟨A⟩ cannot be doubted either as regards another or itself. A should not be doubted as regards another because it is certain that nothing other than A is pro-

---

[117] That is, that A is unknown by you is true, since it was granted by the proponent of this solution.

[118] Again, as in n. 117.

[119] It is only a paralogism if nothing else is proposed to you, in which case 'Something proposed to you is not known by you' and 'Nothing proposed to you is known by you' are equivalent. Suppose A is known by you. Since A was proposed to you, something proposed to you is known by you. But only A was proposed to you. So everything proposed to you is known by you, so A is false. This contradicts the assumption that A is known by you, so by reductio, A is not known by you. So something proposed to you is not known by you, but that is what A signifies, so A is true and you've proved it. So A is known by you. Paradox.

[120] If you grant A, then A is known by you, so since A was proposed to you, something proposed to you is known by you, which contradicts A. So you've granted badly.

> Hoc tibi propositum est tibi dubium, ergo aliquod tibi
> propositum est tibi dubium,

quia arguitur a singulari ad eius indefinitam.

ad 6.12 Ideo dico quod A est falsum nec potest hic deduci ad aliquid
inconveniens nec est hoc insolubile, sicut ut hic proponatur hec:

> Nullum ⟨tibi⟩ propositum est tibi dubium.

Si enim conceditur, nullum inconveniens accidit. Similiter si proponatur

> Hoc tibi propositum est scitum a te,

si conceditur, numquam accidit insolubile.

6.13 Sed in disiunctivis maior est difficultas. Proponatur hec:

> Rex | sedet vel disiunctiva tibi proposita est tibi dubia,   E$_8$ 30vb

que sit A. Non potest concedi quia non pro prima parte nec pro secunda quia tunc secunda est falsa. Nec potest negari eadem ratione. Si dubitetur, tunc sic: A est tibi dubium, ergo disiunctiva tibi proposita est tibi dubia, et hec est secunda pars disiunctive, ergo secunda pars est vera, ergo tota vera.

ad 6.13 Ad illud dico dubitando istam:

> Rex sedet vel disiunctiva tibi proposita est tibi dubia,

et nego consequentiam:

> Ista disiunctiva est tibi dubia, ergo disiunctiva tibi pro-
> posita est tibi dubia,

quia extrema consequentis non supponunt pro A quia ista propositio disiunctiva tibi proposita est tibi dubia nec potest verificari nec denotare seipsam esse veram pro hac disiunctiva, hoc posito quod homo consideret de illa sicut considerare debeat. Et hoc probatur sic. Si enim posset verificari pro A disiunctiva tibi dubia, ergo aliqua disiunctiva tibi proposita est tibi dubia, et antecedens est verum per ypothesim, ergo consequens;

---

3 indefinitam] infinitam E$_4$ 4 dico] dicit O || hic] om. O   7 nullum] enim add. E$_8$
8 Hoc] hec O || tibi] om. E$_4$ p.c.E$_8$ 9 conceditur] concedit O   10 disiunctivis] hec in quibus add. O || maior est] inv. O || Proponatur] proponitur E$_8$ post disiunctivis O   11 tibi proposita] om. E$_4$ 12 parte] tibi sit dubia add. E$_4$ || secunda] parte add. E$_4$ 13 secunda] om. E$_4$ || est] esset O || dubitetur] dubitatur O   14 sic] est E$_4$ || disiunctiva] om. O
15 pars^2] disiunctive add. O || tota] toto E$_4$ est add. O   16 dubitando istam] istud dubito E$_4$ 18–19 et nego ... dubia] om. hom. E$_8$ 19 tibi^2] om. E$_4$ 18–22 et nego ... dubia] om. hom. O   23 seipsam] se E$_4$ O || homo] hoc E$_4$ 24 debeat] debet O || enim] om. O   25 aliqua] consequentia E$_4$ 26 et] om. O || ergo] et add. O

posed to you. And it should not be doubted as regards itself because if the subject supposits for the whole, this inference:

> This, which is proposed to you, is uncertain for you, therefore something proposed to you is uncertain for you,

is valid because it argues from a singular proposition to its indefinite.

ad 6.12 For that reason[121] I reply that A is false and that here one cannot deduce anything inconsistent, nor is this an insoluble, any more than if, for example, this:

> Nothing proposed ⟨to you⟩ is uncertain for you,

is proposed: for if it is granted no inconsistency results. Similarly if:

> This, which is proposed to you, is known by you,

is proposed: if it is granted an insoluble never results.

6.13 But in disjunctions there is a greater difficulty. Let this:

> The king is sitting or a disjunction proposed to you is uncertain for you,

be proposed, call it A.[122] It cannot be granted either as regards the first disjunct, or the second—because then the second is false. Nor can it be denied, for the same reason.[123] If it is doubted, then I argue like this: A is uncertain for you, therefore a disjunction proposed to you is uncertain for you, and this is the second disjunct of the disjunction, therefore the second disjunct is true, therefore the whole disjunction is true.

ad 6.13 To this I reply by expressing doubt about:

> The king is sitting or a disjunction proposed to you is uncertain for you,

and I deny the inference:

> This disjunction is uncertain for you, therefore a disjunction proposed to you is uncertain for you,

because the extremes of the conclusion do not supposit for A, because the disjunctive proposition proposed to you is uncertain for you, and cannot be true about nor mean that it itself is true of this disjunction, provided that someone thought about it as it should be thought about. And this is proved like this. For if 'disjunction uncertain for you' could be true of A, then some disjunction proposed to you is uncertain for you, and

---

[121] Having shown in §6.12 that you can't grant and can't doubt the paralogism, the response is to deny it. It is strange that Segrave does not show that A is a paralogism, as he claimed at the start of §6.12. So he does not apply his diagnosis showing that the paralogism depends on the fallacy of accident.

[122] Cf. Bradwardine, §§9.7.3–9.7.5. Cf. §8.4.

[123] 'The king is sitting' is a standard example in Obligations treatises of a proposition whose truth-value in the scenario is not known.

et consequens est altera pars disiunctive, ergo disiunctiva est vera; et antecedens est verum per ypothesim et scitum a te si consideres, ergo consequens, ergo disiunctiva non est tibi dubia, ergo si verificatur ista propositio:

    Aliqua disiunctiva tibi proposita est tibi dubia

pro A, sequitur quod non verificatur pro illa, ergo illam non supponunt extrema, sicut prius patuit evidenter.

6.13.1 Sed queritur quomodo est hoc insolubile cum hic non ponatur iste terminus 'verum', nec iste terminus 'falsum'.

ad 6.13.1 Ad quod dico quod hic ponitur equivalens, dubium namque est quod est apprehensum nec cognitum esse verum nec scitum esse falsum et ita ponuntur isti termini | implicite licet non explicite. Si autem disiungatur hec propositio:

    Aliqua disiunctiva tibi proposita est tibi dubia,

cum propositione vera tota disiunctiva foret concedenda, si tamen falsa scita esse falsa foret neganda nec accideret insolubile. Si etiam poneretur hec:

    Rex sedet vel nulla disiunctiva tibi proposita est tibi dubia,

si hec conceditur, numquam accidit insolubile, sicut responsum est. Ad hec consimiliter et ad omnia similia respondendum est.

6.14 Aliter paralogizatur sic: sit A altera istarum:

    ⟨D⟩ Deus est,

et

    ⟨C⟩ Nullum propositum sorti est scitum a te,

et lateat te que illarum sit A.

Et proponatur ista sorti ⟨et nulla alia⟩:

    ⟨B⟩ A est scitum a te,

et queratur de ista:

    ⟨B⟩ A est scitum a te,

---

1 consequens] antecedens O   2 consideres] consideras E$_8$ 5 disiunctiva] om. E$_4$ E$_8$ 6 pro^1] per E$_4$ || supponunt] supponit E$_4$ E$_8$ 7 prius] om. E$_8$ O   8 est hoc] inv. O   9 nec iste terminus] vel O   10 quod^1] hoc O   11 cognitum] scitum O   12 et ita] si O   13 disiungatur corr.] distinguatur E$_8$ O distinguetur E$_4$ || hec] ista O   16 foret] esset O || accideret] accidet E$_8$ || etiam] enim O   18 proposita] dicta add. O   20 accidit] accidet E$_8$ 21 consimiliter] post similia O || est] om. E$_4$ E$_8$ 26 te] om. E$_4$ E$_8$ || illarum] illorum E$_8$ || sit A] om. E$_4$ E$_8$ 27 proponatur] proponitur E$_4$ || et nulla alia coniecimus ex fontis (Kilvington, Bradwardine)] om. mss

the premise[124] is true by hypothesis, therefore the conclusion ⟨is true as well⟩; and the conclusion is one disjunct of the disjunction, therefore the disjunction is true; and the premise[125] is true by hypothesis and known by you if you think about it, therefore so too is the conclusion; therefore the disjunction is not uncertain for you, therefore if this proposition:

> Some disjunction proposed to you is uncertain for you

is true about A, it follows that it is not true about it, therefore the extremes do not supposit for it, as was manifestly clear before.

6.13.1 But one may ask in what way this is an insoluble, since the term 'true' does not appear here nor the term 'false'.

ad 6.13.1 To this I reply that a term equivalent to these does appear here, for what is uncertain is understood as what is neither recognized to be true nor known to be false, and so the terms ⟨'true' and 'false'⟩ appear implicitly, although not explicitly. If this proposition

> Some disjunction proposed to you is uncertain for you

is disjoined with a true proposition ⟨known to be true⟩, the whole disjunction should be granted. If however it is disjoined with a false proposition known to be false, the whole disjunction should be denied and no insoluble results. And if:

> The king is sitting or no disjunction proposed to you is uncertain for you,

is proposed: if it is granted, an insoluble never results, as in the previous response. One should respond to this and to all similar propositions likewise.

6.14 A paralogism may be made in another way like this: let A be one of these:

> ⟨D⟩ God exists,

and

> ⟨C⟩ Nothing proposed to Socrates is known by you,

where it is unknown to you which of these is A.
And let the proposition:

> ⟨B⟩ A is known by you,

be proposed to Socrates ⟨and nothing else⟩ and ask about:

> ⟨B⟩ A is known by you

---

[124] *Sc.* "'disjunction uncertain for you' could be true of A".
[125] *Sc.* "the conclusion is one disjunct of the disjunction". Segrave is here ignoring the difference between 'a disjunction' and 'some disjunction'.

utrum sit vera vel falsa.

6.14.1 ⟨B⟩ negari non potest, quia sequitur:

> A est 'Deus est', ergo A est scitum a te.

Antecedens est dubium, ergo consequens non est negandum.

6.14.2 Nec est hoc ⟨B⟩ dubitandum quia sequitur:

> Hoc propositum sorti est tibi dubium, ergo hoc non est scitum a te,

et sequitur ultra:

> Hoc propositum sorti non est scitum a te, ergo nullum propositum sorti est scitum a te.

Consequentia patet quia tantum hec est proposita sorti; et antecedens est scitum a te, ergo consequens. Et tunc arguitur sic:

> Hec est scita a te: Nullum propositum sorti est scitum a te, et: Deus est est scita a te, ergo utrumque istorum est scitum a te; A est alterum istorum, ergo A est scitum a te.

6.14.3 Tunc concedo istam:

> ⟨B⟩ A est scitum | a te.

Qua concessa proponatur hec:

> ⟨C⟩ Nullum propositum sorti est scitum a te.

6.14.3.1 Hoc negari non potest quia sequitur: |

> Hec est falsa, et hec est A, ergo A est falsum,

et ultra:

> Ergo A non est scitum a te.

30–1 a te utrum] aut O   1 vel] aut est O   4 non est] add. in marg. E₄   3–4 Deus ... est] ergo aliquid est, ergo Deus est. Ista consequentia est bona, scita a te esse bona, et antecedens est scitum a te, ergo et consequens non est tibi dubium, ergo consequens non est a te O   6 hoc] om. O   8 ultra] ulterius O   9 nullum] se add. E₄   11 patet] apparet E₄   12 ergo] et add. O   ‖ Et] om. O   13 Hec] hoc O   ‖ scita] scitum O om. E₄ et add. O   14 Deus] del. p.c. E₄   ‖ est¹] om. E₄ E₈   ‖ scita] scitum E₈ O   ‖ istorum] istarum O   15 scitum¹] scita O   ‖ te¹] et add. O   ‖ istorum] istarum O   ‖ te²] et add. O   16 Tunc] om. E₄   17 a te] om. E₄ O   18 Qua] contra E₈   19 sorti] om. O   20 sequitur] ergo add. O   21 Hec] ergo O   ‖ falsa] falsum O   ‖ hec] hoc E₈   22 ultra] ulterius O   23 a te] om. O

whether it is true or false.[126]

6.14.1[127] ⟨B⟩ cannot be denied because the inference:

> A is 'God exists', therefore A is known by you,

is valid. The premise is uncertain, therefore the conclusion should not be denied.[128]

6.14.2[129] Nor should ⟨B⟩ be doubted, because the inference:

> This, which is proposed to Socrates, is uncertain for you, therefore this is not known by you,

is valid, and moreover this is valid:

> This, which is proposed to Socrates, is not known by you, therefore nothing proposed to Socrates is known by you.

The validity of the latter inference is clear because only ⟨B⟩ is proposed to Socrates; and the premise is known by you, therefore the conclusion ⟨is known by you⟩. And then one argues like this:

> 'Nothing proposed to Socrates is known by you' ⟨sc. C⟩ is known by you, and 'God exists' is known by you, therefore each of them is known by you; A is one of these, therefore A is known by you.

6.14.3[130] Then I grant:

> ⟨B⟩ A is known by you.

Once ⟨B⟩ is granted, let

> ⟨C⟩ Nothing proposed to Socrates is known by you be proposed.

6.14.3.1 ⟨C⟩ cannot be denied because the inference:

> This is false, and this is A, therefore A is false,

is valid, and furthermore:

> Therefore A is not known by you

---

[126] See Kilvington, *Sophismata*, sophism 48, and Bradwardine, *Insolubilia*, Appendix A, §A.1 (with 'concessum' in place of 'propositum'). Kilvington and Bradwardine add that only B is granted by Socrates ('et nulla alia'), and Segrave's argument at §6.14.3.2 assumes this. Segrave introduces the designation 'B' for 'A is known by you' in §6.14.3.3 below (following Kilvington—it's called 'D' by Bradwardine, who dubs 'God exists' B). John Dumbleton also claims in his *Summa Logicae*, ch. 25 (part of his 'De Scire'), without spelling it out, that his solution solves it.

[127] Cf. Kilvington, *Sophismata*, S48(e), where Kilvington shows that the sophismatic proposition, B, cannot be denied; also Bradwardine §A.1.2.

[128] Again, use of Kilvington's disputational meta-argument. See n. 104 above.

[129] Cf. Kilvington, *Sophismata*, S48(c), where Kilvington shows that B cannot be doubted; also Bradwardine, *Inoslubilia*, §A.1.3.

[130] Cf. Kilvington, *Sophismata*, S48(d), where Kilvington shows that B cannot be granted; also Bradwardine, *Insolubilia*, §§A.1.1–A.1.1.3.

Consequentia est bona, et antecedens est dubium, ergo consequens non est negandum; tamen consequens est falsum quia concessisti quod A est scitum a te.

6.14.3.2 Similiter nec dubitari potest ⟨C⟩ quia sequitur:

Hec est tibi dubia et hec est A, ergo A est tibi dubium.

Consequens est falsum quia A est scitum a te.

6.14.3.3 Ideo concedo istam similiter

⟨C⟩ Nullum propositum sorti est scitum a te.

Sed arguitur tunc sic:

⟨E⟩ Nullum propositum sorti est scitum a te, B est propositum sorti, ergo B non est scitum a te,

(sit B ista 'A est scitum a te'). Consequens est falsum quia B est scitum a te et concessum.

ad 6.14 Ideo dubito istam consequentiam ⟨E⟩, quia si A sit hec:

⟨C⟩ Nullum propositum sorti est scitum a te,

consequentia ⟨E⟩ non valet; si sit

⟨D⟩ Deus est,

consequentia ⟨E⟩ bona est.

Et similiter dubito consequentiam ex opposito, hanc videlicet:

⟨E'⟩ B est scitum a te, et B est propositum sorti, ergo aliquod propositum sorti est scitum a te,

quia si A sit ista:

---

2 tamen consequens] *inv.* E$_4$ || est^2] *om.* E$_4$ E$_8$ 5 Hec] hoc O || dubia] dubium O || hec] hoc O || A^2] *om.* E$_4$ E$_8$ 6 est^1] *om.* E$_4$ E$_8$ || te] et *add.* O   12 A] *om.* E$_4$ 13 concessum] et *add.* O   18 consequentia] *om. p.c* E$_4$ 19 dubito] *om.* O || videlicet] scilicet O   21 aliquod] aliquid O

follows. The inference is valid and the ⟨second⟩ premise (ʼThis is Aʼ) is uncertain, so the conclusion should not be denied;[131] yet the conclusion is false because ⟨in §6.14.1.3⟩ you have granted that A is known by you.

6.14.3.2 Similarly, ⟨C⟩ cannot be doubted because the inference:

> This is uncertain for you and this is A, therefore A is uncertain for you,

is valid. The conclusion is false because A is known by you.[132]

6.14.3.3[133] So I also grant:

> ⟨C⟩ Nothing proposed to Socrates is known by you.

But then one argues like this:

> ⟨E⟩ Nothing proposed to Socrates is known by you, B is proposed to Socrates, therefore B is not known by you,

where B is 'A is known by you'. The conclusion is false because B is known and was granted by you ⟨in §6.14.1.3⟩.[134]

ad 6.14 So I question the validity of inference ⟨E⟩ because if A is:

> ⟨C⟩ Nothing proposed to Socrates is known by you,

inference ⟨E⟩ is not valid; while if ⟨A⟩ is:

> ⟨D⟩ God exists,

inference ⟨E⟩ is valid.[135]

And similarly, I question the validity of the inference drawn from the opposite ⟨of E's conclusion⟩,[136] namely:

> ⟨E´⟩ B is known by you and B is proposed to Socrates, therefore something proposed to Socrates is known by you,[137]

because if A is:

---

[131] Again, note the use of Kilvington's disputational meta-argument.
[132] Presumably, 'this' in §§6.14.3.1–2 refers to C. Note that, given the correction of the scenario to specify that only B is proposed to Socrates (see n. 116), C is equivalent to 'B is not known by you'.
[133] Cf. Bradwardine, *Insolubilia*, §A.1.1.1, where he introduces inference E. 'E' is Bradwardine's designation for the inference.
[134] To complete the sophism: the minor premise is given in the scenario, so the major premise, that is, C, cannot be granted. So C cannot be denied, doubted or granted, and so B cannot be granted, as it was in §6.14.1.3. So B cannot be denied, doubted or granted.
[135] If A is C, E commits a fallacy of accident, for in that case, in the first premise 'is known by you' cannot supposit for A, while it does in the conclusion; while if A is 'God exists', E is valid but its first premise is false, as is its conclusion.
[136] ⟨E⟩ and ⟨E´⟩ are equivalent by the rule that "when there are many premises [...] it is necessary that from the opposite of the consequent with one premise the opposite of the other premise follows" (Ockham, *Summa Logicae*, III-3 ch. 38: "[...] quando antecedens continet plures propositiones [...] oportet quod ex opposito consequentis cum una propositionum sequatur oppositum alterius propositionis").
[137] Cf. Kilvington, *Sophismata*, S48(k).

⟨C⟩ Nullum propositum sorti est scitum a te,

tunc in ista:

Aliquod propositum sorti est scitum a te,

extrema non supponunt pro B quia si supponerent pro B esset scitum, cum B antecedat ad contradictorium huius:

Aliquod propositum sorti est scitum a te,

ista significaret suum contradictorium esse verum et ita significaret se esse veram pro suo contradictorio vero, quod non potest. Et ita patet quod similiter in ista:

⟨C⟩ Nullum propositum sorti est scitum | a te E₈ 31va

subiectum non supponit pro B, cum A significaret istam:

Nullum propositum sorti est scitum a te.

Ex illo dicto patet quomodo sit respondendum ad talia sophysmata.

6.15 Ponatur quod tantum iste due propositiones:

Deus est,

et

Deus est ⟨est⟩ maxima propositio vera,

que sit A, et queratur an A sit vera vel falsa.

---

4 esset] essent E₈   5 cum] cum *vel* tamen (*dub.*) E₄   9 similiter] sicut O   13 illo dicto] illa dicta E₄ || talia] *om.* O   14 Ponatur] proponatur E₈ O   16 et] *om.* O   17 maxima] maxime E₈ O   18 falsa] vera E₈

⟨C⟩ Nothing proposed to Socrates is known by you,

then in:

Something proposed to Socrates is known by you

the extremes do not supposit for B because if they did supposit for B, ⟨'Something proposed to Socrates is known by you'⟩ would be known.[138] But, since B implies the contradictory of:

Something proposed to Socrates is known by you,

⟨which is the contradictory of C⟩, this proposition would signify that its contradictory ⟨sc. C⟩ was true and so it would signify itself to be true about its true contradictory ⟨C⟩, which cannot be the case. And so it is clear that also in:

⟨C⟩ Nothing proposed to Socrates is known by you,

the subject does not supposit for B, since A would signify this:

Nothing proposed to Socrates is known by you.

It is clear from what has been said how one should respond to these sophisms.

6.15 Let us suppose that there are only these two propositions:

God exists,

and

'God exists' is the greatest true proposition,[139]

call ⟨the latter⟩ A, and ask if A is true or false.[140]

---

[138] That is, inference ⟨E'⟩ would be valid, and so the conclusion would be known since the premises are known.

[139] Another possible interpretation of 'maxima propositio' is as a maxim (see, e.g., Boethius, *De Topicis Differentiis*, tr. Stump, pp. 33, 46 ff.), but it's not clear that this is the interpretation of the phrase that Bradwardine and Segrave are alluding to here.

[140] See Bradwardine, *Insolubilia*, §12.1, who dubs 'God exists' A and '"God exists" is the greatest true proposition' B. Bradwardine proves that 'God exists' is "the truest principle of all" (*verissimum omnium*) in his *De Causa Dei*, ed. Savile, I 11 (1618, 199A): "Moreover, in the order of truths, there is no infinite regress, but there is some first truth which is the cause of all others. But it is this, 'God exists', since this does not have any truth as its prior cause" (Item in ordine verorum non est infinitus processus; sed est aliquod primum verum, quod est causa omnium aliorum. Sed illud est, Deus est, cum non habeat aliquod verum prius causam illius). See also §6.9 above. Staying with Segrave's terminology, suppose that A (that is '"God exists" is the greatest true proposition') is true. Then no proposition is more true than 'God exists', but A entails that 'God exists' is true (and not vice versa) and so is greater (more true) than it. Contradiction. So A is not true but false, in which case 'God exists' is not the greatest true proposition. But A is the only other proposition so it must be greater and true. Paradox. (Note that this proof of paradox starts with the inference which Segrave then rejects in §ad 6.15.)

ad 6.15 Et patet ex dictis quod A est concedenda, et non sequitur:

>A est vera, et A est maior quam deus est, ergo deus est non est maxima ⟨propositio vera⟩.

Causa autem quare non sequitur eadem est in omnibus.

6.16 Similiter sit A nomen cuiuslibet propositionis cuius predicatum est vere predicabile de toto, et B nomen cuiuslibet propositionis cuius predicatum vere non | dicitur de toto cuius est ⟨pars⟩, tunc

>Homo est animal est B.

Hec est vera et sit illa C, queritur utrum C sit A vel B, et patet deductio sicut in aliis.

ad 6.16 Ad illud dicitur quod C est B, et cum dicitur:

>C est B, et B est predicatum ipsius C, ergo predicatum ipsius C vere dicitur de C, ergo C est A,

negatur hec consequentia:

>B dicitur de C vere, et B est predicatum ipsius C, ergo predicatum ipsius C vere dicitur de C,

quia in consequente subiectum non supponit pro B. Non enim potest denotare se esse veram sine contradictione pro hoc predicato B, sicut patet inspicienti, ideo pro illo non supponit, sed est sensus:

>Predicatum C non vere dicitur de C.

6.17 Sic ergo ex predictis patet quomodo respondendum sit ad omne insolubile.

---

1 est] sit O   2 et] *om.* O   4 quare] quia O   5 nomen cuiuslibet] nullum predicatum alicuius O   ‖ predicatum] non vere dicitur de toto *add. a.c.* E$_8$ 6–7 est ... predicatum] *om. hom.* O   7 vere non] *inv.* E$_8$ 9 et^1] *om.* E$_4$ 11 dicitur^2] arguitur E$_4$ 11–12 et ... B] *om. hom.* O   12 C^2] A *in marg.* O   12–13 ergo ... vere] *om. hom.* E$_4$ 13 dicitur] predicatur O ‖ C est A] A est C O   15 dicitur] *om.* E$_4$ 15–16 ipsius ... predicatum] *om. hom.* E$_4$ 15 C^2] *om.* E$_8$ 16 predicatum ipsius C] *om. hom.* O   17 consequente] antecedente E$_8$ 21 Sic] ecce O   ‖ respondendum sit] *inv.* O   ‖ omne] *om.* O   22 insolubile] etc. stude quia proderit multum *add.* O

ad 6.15 And it is clear from what has been said that A should be granted, and this is not valid:

> A is true and A is greater than 'God exists', therefore 'God exists' is not the greatest ⟨true proposition⟩.

And the reason why it is not valid is the same in every case.

6.16 Similarly, let A be the ⟨common⟩ name of any proposition whose predicate is truly predicable of the whole, and B be the ⟨common⟩ name of any proposition whose predicate is not truly said of the whole of which it is part.[141] Then consider:

> 'A man is an animal' is a B,

This is true. Call it C and ask if C is an A or a B, and the argument is clear, just as in the other cases.[142]

ad 6.16 To this I reply that C is a B, and when it is said:

> C is a B and B is C's predicate, therefore C's predicate is truly said of C, therefore C is an A,

I deny the following inference:

> B is truly said of C and B is ⟨C's⟩ predicate, therefore C's predicate is truly said of C,

because in the conclusion the subject does not supposit for B. For it cannot mean that it itself is true of this predicate B without contradiction, as is clear to anyone who considers this, so it does not supposit for ⟨B⟩. But the sense ⟨of 'C is a B'⟩ is:

> C's predicate is not truly said of C.

6.17 So, from what has been said it is clear how one should respond to every insoluble.

---

[141] 'A' is somewhat like the predicate 'autological', and 'B' is somewhat like 'heterological'. Cf. Grelling's paradox (q.v.). Note that A and B are contradictory predicates, so every proposition must be either an A or a B and not both.

[142] If C is an A, then C's predicate is truly said of C, and B is C's predicate, so C is a B; while if C is a B, then since B is C's predicate, C's predicate is truly said of C, so C is an A. But it must be either an A or a B, so it's both. Contradiction. See Bradwardine, *Insolubilia*, §§10.1–2, and discussion, *ibid.*, 'Introduction', p. 9.

⟨Capitulum Septimum⟩
⟨De apparentibus insolubilibus⟩

7.1 | Iam restat quedam alia sophysmata solvere que apparent insolubilia, non tamen sunt, ut hec:

7.1.1 Ponatur quod ista scribatur:

>Hoc est verum,

que sit A, et hec similiter:

>Hoc est falsum,

que sit B; et ponatur quod per subiectum ipsius A demonstretur B et per subiectum B demonstretur A. Queritur tunc aut A sit verum vel falsum. Si verum, cum non significet nisi B esse verum, ergo B esse verum est verum, ergo B est verum, et B significat A esse falsum, ergo A esse falsum est verum, ergo A est falsum. Si conceditur quod A est falsum, ergo B est falsum. Consequentia satis patet et sequitur: B est falsum, ergo A esse falsum est falsum, ergo A non est falsum.

7.1.2 Simile est: significet A B esse falsum et B C esse falsum et C A esse falsum, et accidit | idem.

7.1.3 Similiter: significet A istam:

>Hoc non est verum,

et queratur an A sit verum vel falsum.

ad 7.1 In omnibus hiis est eadem solutio. Pro quo est sciendum primo quid est significare; ut vult Aristoteles in libro Peryhermenias capitulo de verbo, significare est intellectum constituere in animo audientis et eius animum sistere et quietare et representare aliquid. Dicit enim sic:

>ipsa quidem secundum se dicta nomina verba sunt et significant aliquid; constituit enim qui dicit intellectum et qui audit quiescit.

Illud ergo nomen significat aliquid quod sistit et quietat intellectum in illo et hoc indifferenter quantum est ex parte sua et etiam quocumque

---

3 Iam] nunc O ‖ sophysmata] *om.* O ‖ que] quia tamen E₄   4 non tamen sunt] non sunt E₈ *om.* E₄   ‖ ut] sicut O ‖ hec] hic E₄ O   5 Ponatur] ponitur E₈   9 demonstretur] demonstratur E₈   10 demonstretur] demonstratur E₈ ‖ sit] est O   11 verum¹] falsum E₄ ‖ esse² verum³] est verum *scr. et del.* E₄   12 esse²] est E₄   14 sequitur] scitur E₈ ‖ est] esse E₈   16 est] hoc si *add.* O   19 Hoc] *om.* E₄ E₈   20 an] utrum E₄   21 est²] *om.* E₄ O   22 est] sit O ‖ vult Aristoteles] Philosophus vult O ‖ in libro] libro E₄ primo O   23 significare] *om.* E₄ ‖ animo] auditoris vel *add.* O   24 aliquid] *om.* E₄ E₈ ‖ Dicit] dico E₄ ‖ sic] *om.* E₄   25 quidem secundum se] *post* verba O   ‖ quidem] quid E₄ enim quod O ‖ nomina] et *add.* E₄ vel *add.* E₈ O ‖ sunt] *om. p.c.* E₄   26 enim] quod E₄ *om.* E₈   29 sua] intelligit quodcumque *add.* E₄ intelligit cuicumque *add.* O ‖ etiam] aliquo O

⟨Chapter 7⟩

⟨On merely apparent insolubles⟩

7.1 It now remains to solve some sophisms which seem to be but are not insolubles, such as these:

7.1.1 Suppose that someone writes:

> This is true,

call it A, and also

> This is false,

call it B.[143] And suppose that A's subject refers to B and B's subject refers to A. Then ask if A is true or false. If ⟨A⟩ is true then, since it signifies only that B is true, it is true that B is true, therefore B is true; and B signifies ⟨only⟩ that A is false, therefore it is true that A is false, therefore A is false. If it is granted that A is false, then B is false. The inference is clear enough and then: from 'B is false' it follows that it is false that A is false, therefore A is not false.

7.1.2 A similar one: let A signify that B is false and let B signify that C is false and C that A is false, and the same thing happens.

7.1.3 Similarly: let A signify:

> This is not true,[144]

and ask if A is true or false.

ad 7.1 The solution is the same in all these cases. Here first recall what it is to signify: as Aristotle proposes in *De Interpretatione* ch. ⟨3⟩, 'On Verbs', to signify is to establish a thought in the hearer's mind[145] and to make their mind come to a halt and acquiesce and to represent something ⟨to their mind⟩. For he says this:

> "Verbs taken by themselves are names and signify something; for the speaker establishes a thought and the hearer settles on it."[146]

Therefore, that name signifies something which it presents and it brings the thought to rest on it, and this indifferently for its own part and also

---

[143] See Bradwardine, *Insolubilia*, §4.2.3. (Bradwardine's own solution is given in §ad 4.2.3 in ch. 12, p. 168.)

[144] See Bradwardine, *Insolubilia*, §4.2.4. (Again, Bradwardine's own solution is given in §ad 4.2.4 in ch. 12, p. 170.)

[145] Hamesse, *Les auctoritates Aristotelis*, p. 305, #6.

[146] Aristotle, *De interpretatione*, ch. 3, 16b20; in Boethius' translation: "Ipsa quidem secundum se dicta verba nomina sunt et significant aliquid—constituit enim qui dicit intellectum, et qui audit quiescit" (*De Interpretatione vel Periermenias*, p. 7)

alio intellecto; non enim | est vox agens ⟨cognoscens⟩, sed quantum est ex parte sua semper uno modo agit. Unde si Sortes per aliquam propositionem aliquando voluntarie intelligit verum et solum verum, non tamen propter hoc dicitur propositio significare illud verum ex quo [significare] debeat propositio dici vera, sed illud dicitur propositio significare ad cuius intellectum actualem semper movet audientem et hoc quantum in eo est et hoc indifferenter quemcumque audientem, quacumque alia intellecta. Potest enim homo voluntarie per istam:

Homo est animal

intelligere hominem esse asinum, sed tamen illud non significat.

ad 7.1.1 Isto supposito dico quod iste due orationes:

Hoc est verum

et

Hoc est falsum

possunt dupliciter considerari. Uno modo materialiter, alio modo significative. Materialiter accepte nihil significant nisi se ipsas et hoc non per modum complexi sed incomplexi ut lignum, lapis, se ipsas significant. Dico ergo quod subiectum ipsius A potest demonstrare vel singulariter significare ipsum B materialiter acceptum; potest enim intellectum eius constituere sic et animum audientis in ipso quietare. Et similiter e converso, subiectum ipsius B sic potest significare A. Et si sic significet, non est difficultas, quia constat quod utrumque istorum significative acceptum est falsum, quia A significat B materialiter acceptum fore verum et hoc est falsum; similiter B acceptum significative significat A materialiter acceptum esse falsum et hoc similiter est falsum, quia neutrum illorum materialiter acceptum est verum | vel falsum.

Si autem in hac institutione sic instituatur ut per utriusque subiectum demonstretur alterum acceptum significative, dico quod hoc est impos-

---

1 enim est] *inv.* O || cognoscens *coniecimus*] vel cognitionis cognoscere E_4 *a.c.*E_8 cuiuscumque vel cognitionis cognoscere *p.c.* E_8 vel cognitionis cognoscit O || sed] in *add.* E_4 1–2 ex parte] extra E_4 2 semper uno modo] uno modo semper O || aliquam] aliam E_4 3 aliquando] oculo O || tamen] *post* propositio O 4 propter] ex E_4 5 debeat] debebat O || illud] igitur E_4 6 actualem] intellectualius E_4 7 est] *om.* O || quemcumque] quantum E_4 || audientem] et in *add.* O 7–8 quacumque ... intellecta] quamcumque aliam intellectam E_4 7 quacumque] re *add.* O 8 istam] idem E_4 10 sed] *om.* O || tamen illud non] illud non tamen E_4 11 dico] *om.* E_4 15 alio modo] et E_4 16 accepte] accepta E_4 E_8 || ipsas] ipsa O 18 subiectum] significatum E_4 || demonstrare] denominare O ipsum *add.* E_4 || singulariter] formam O 19 intellectum eius] *inv.* E_4 20 constituere sic] *inv.* O || et animum] in animo E_4 animam O || in ipso] et enim ipsam O || quietare] quietatur E_4 || similiter] sic O 20–21 converso] contra *a.c.*E_4 E_8 21 subiectum] significatum E_4 || sic^1] *om.* E_4 || significet] significat O 23 A] *om.* O sic *add.* E_4 || significat] significabit O 25 esse] fore O || similiter] simili O 26 est verum] *inv.* E_4 27 instituatur] instituantur E_8 || per utriusque] pro utroque E_8 O 28 demonstretur] denotaretur et O

regardless of any other thing comprehended; for a sound does not have a mind of its own, but for its own part always acts in the same way. Thus if Socrates at some time wilfully comprehends a truth and only a truth by some proposition, it is not for that reason, however, that the proposition is said to signify that truth from which the proposition should be said to be true. But the proposition is said to signify that towards whose actual comprehension ⟨the proposition⟩ always prompts the hearer, and ⟨it does⟩ this in itself and does this for any hearer indifferently regardless of any other thing comprehended. For by:

A man is an animal,

a man can wilfully comprehend that a man is an ass, and yet it does not signify that.

ad 7.1.1 Having assumed that, I reply that these two utterances:

This is true,

and

This is false,

⟨which we called A and B respectively⟩ can be thought about in two ways, in one way materially, in another way significatively.[147] Taken materially ⟨the utterances⟩ only signify themselves and this not in a propositionally complex way but, just like 'wood stone', they signify themselves in a non-propositional way. Therefore I reply that A's subject can refer to or individually signify B taken materially, for it can establish ⟨the speaker's⟩ thought of it ⟨sc. B⟩ in this way and bring the hearer's mind to settle on it. And similarly, conversely, B's subject can signify A taken in this way ⟨sc. materially⟩. And if it signifies it in that way, there is no difficulty, because it is certain that each of these utterances taken significatively is false, because A signifies that B taken materially is true and this is false; similarly, B taken significatively signifies that A taken materially is false and this is false too, because neither of them taken materially is true or false.

However, if in this manner it is so established that by the subject of each utterance the other utterance is referred to taken significatively, I reply

---

[147] See, e.g., Ockham, *Summa Logicae*, I 64, p. 196: "material supposition is when the term does not supposit significatively" (suppositio materialis est quando terminus non supponat significative); Buridan, *Sophismata*, ed. Pironet, p. 56: "To the third sophism ('Man is a species') one can respond [...] by saying that the sophism is true taking the term 'man' materially, and false taking it personally or significatively" (Ad tertium sophisma ('homo est species'), potest responderi [...] dicendo quod sophisma est verum, capiendo istum terminum 'homo' materialiter, et falsum, capiendo personaliter sive significative). See also Manlevelt, *Quaestiones libri Porphyrii*, p. 212, where he observes that although all personal supposition is significative, not all significative supposition is personal.

sibile. Numquam enim erit intellectus audientis per ea quietatus et hoc indifferenter respectu cuiuscumque audientis et quocumque alio intellecto. Significatio enim utriusque dependet ex significatione reliqui et ita quelibet cognitio quam faciunt semper est dependens et ita numquam erit intellectus eiusdem quietatus per ista.

7.1.1.1 Sed forte arguitur: nomina relativa significant aliquid et tamen significata dependent ex se invicem.

ad 7.1.1.1 Ad illud dicendum quod non est simile quia hoc est proprium relativis quod neutrum cognoscatur sine reliquo, sed in proposito non manifestatur aliqua dependentia relativa.

Vel dicitur aliter quod licet significatum termini relativi ut tale dependeat ex suo correlato et e contra, istum tamen terminum significare suum significatum non dependet ex significare alium terminum suum significatum, sed uterque significat significatum suum, ac si alius terminus non significaret, licet secundum tale esse unum representatum non posset prius cognosci sine alio cognito; ita tamen non est in proposito, sed utrumque terminum significare dependet ex reliquum significare.

7.1.1.2 Sed dices forte quod illud non oportet quia pono quod per subiectum ipsius A demonstretur B; et hoc: A, absolute nec materialiter nec significative acceptum. Quo posito stat | argumentum ut prius. E_8 32va

ad 7.1.1.2 Ad illud dicendum quod si A demonstretur, necessario demonstratur significative acceptum vel materialiter acceptum quia inter has acceptiones non est medium, sicut inter significare et non significare non cadit medium. Multotiens tamen consideratur terminus per intentionem communiorem quam sit illa intentio: significare vel quam sit ista intentio: non significare, et tamen in ista necessario consideratur vel significative acceptum vel non significative acceptum. Unde potest terminus

---

1 intellectus ... quietatus] audientis intellectus quietatus per illam E_8 O   2 respectu] om. E_4 E_8 3 Significatio] significatum O   4 ita] ideo O om. E_4 5 intellectus eiusdem] animus O   6 arguitur] aliqua O || aliquid] aliqua E_4 7 significata] significatio O || ex] ad E_4 8 dicendum] dico O   9 neutrum] unum non O   11 quod licet significatum] hee significent O || termini relativi] nominis relatum (dub.) E_4 || tale] tali O || dependeat] dependentiam E_8 dependentiam add. E_4 12 suo] sui O || correlato] correlatio O || e contra] extra E_8 O || significare] significet O   13 significare alium terminum] alio termino significare E_4 significante aliquem terminum O   14 significat] om. O || significatum] om. E_4 E_8 15 secundum tale esse] significatum (dub.) E_4 || posset] om. E_8 || prius] perfecte E_4 om. O   16 cognosci] per alium vel add. O   17 reliquum corr.] reliquo mss   18 pono quod] om. E_8 19 demonstretur] demonstraretur E_4 || A^2] om. O B add. E_4 20 acceptum] post materialiter E_4 || ut] sicut E_4 21 dicendum] dicitur E_4 dico O || demonstretur] demonstraretur E_8 demonstratur O   23 has] duas add. O || acceptiones] expositiones E_4 || sicut] nec add. E_4 E_8 24 consideratur] medium sive O   25 significare] significans E_4 E_8 26 intentio] om. O || et tamen in ista] illa tamen E_4 tamen intentio illa O || vel] post necessario E_4 27 $acceptum^2$] accepta O om. E_4

that this is impossible. For the hearer's thought will never be settled by means of these ⟨subjects⟩ and this indifferently for any hearer and regardless of whatever other thing is comprehended. For the signification of each utterance depends on the signification of the other and so any cognition which the utterances produce is always dependent and so the hearers' comprehension will never be settled by means of these ⟨subjects⟩.

7.1.1.1 But perhaps one can argue that relatives[148] signify something and yet their significates depend on each other.

ad 7.1.1.1 To this it should be replied that the two cases are not similar because it is peculiar to relatives that neither of them is known without the other, but in the present case no relative dependency is evidenced.

Alternatively, one might reply that although the significate of a relative term as such depends on its correlate and vice versa, yet one term's signifying its own significate does not depend on the other term's signifying its significate. What is more, each ⟨relative term⟩ signifies its own significate even if the other term did not signify it; although according to such being, the one thing represented ⟨to the mind⟩ could not be known earlier without the other being known. However it is not so in the case ⟨of A and B⟩, but each term's signifying depends on the other's signifying.

7.1.1.2 But perhaps you may reply that this is not necessary because I assume ⟨as in 7.1.1⟩ that B is referred to by A's subject; and A is taken neither materially nor significatively but absolutely.[149] Having assumed that, the argument works as before.

ad 7.1.1.2 To this it should be replied that if A is referred to, it is necessarily referred to taken either significatively or materially, because there is no middle between these ways of taking it, just as there is no middle between signifying and not signifying. However, often a term is thought about by means of an intention more general than the intention of signifying, or than the intention of not signifying, yet it is necessarily thought about in it taken either significatively or not significatively. Thus a term taken

---

[148] Segrave is not referring to relatives such as 'father/son', 'master/slave', but to anaphora (relative pronouns). On the medieval discussion of anaphora, see, e.g., Parsons, *Articulating Medieval Logic*, ch. 8.

[149] On absolute supposition, see, e.g., *Tractatus de Proprietatibus Sermonum* (in De Rijk, *Logica Modernorum*, II 2, p. 716): "some ⟨modes⟩ of supposition are absolute, some ⟨context-⟩relative. A term is said to have absolute ⟨supposition⟩ when used by itself, e.g., 'man'. For it supposits absolutely from its imposition for anything equally" (suppositionum alia absoluta, alia respectiva. Absoluta dicitur quam habet terminus per se sumptus, ut 'homo'. Supponit enim absolute ex institutione pro quolibet equaliter). It was often called 'suppositio naturalis': see Barth, *The Logic of the Articles in Traditional Philosophy*, ch. 4 §14 (p. 98); De Rijk, 'The Development of Suppositio Naturalis in Medieval Logic', p. 71.

demonstrari significative acceptus, etsi non demonstretur hoc sic dicendo: significative acceptum. Unde sic dicendo:

    Hoc est vox,

demonstrando hanc vocem: homo, si vero ut materialiter acceptam, dico quod demonstretur significative accepta etsi non demonstretur sub hac intentione: significative accepta. Unde est idem dicere:

    hec vox,

et:

    hec vox significans animal rationale,

et ita est in proposito. Unde nullo modo potest esse mutua demonstratio nisi accipiendo demonstrata materialiter quia qualitercumque aliter demonstrarentur, demonstrantur ipsa significata. Et in tali casu numquam posset intellectus eius determinari circa illa significata, ymmo foret circulatio | in infinitum ponendo semper significatum pronominis loco pronominis, sicut manifeste patet sic dicto: O 3ra

    Hoc est verum,

idem foret dicere et dicere sic:

    Hoc est falsum est verum

et loco huius pronominis | ponatur suum significatum sic   E$_4$ 161vb

    Hoc est verum est falsum est verum.

Et ita numquam terminaretur intellectus, ymmo continue terminus unius esset terminus alterius.

ad 7.1.1.2–1 Vel aliter dicitur quod licet per subiectum utriusque possit reliquum significari et hoc absolute neque | ut materialiter neque ut   E$_8$ 32vb
significative, tamen subiectum A non supponit pro B nisi materialiter acceptum. Non enim potest A denotare se esse veram pro B accepta significative sine contradictione et ideo restringitur ne supponat pro B sic

---

1 significative] significare E$_4$ || demonstretur] demonstrative E$_8$ || hoc] hec E$_4$ 3 Hoc] homo E$_8$ 4 vero ut] non demonstretur E$_4$ || materialiter] materia O || acceptam] accepta E$_8$ O   5 demonstretur^1] demonstratur dico quod demonstratur nec O nec *add.* E$_4$ || demonstretur^2] demonstratur O   6 significative accepta] significatum E$_4$ E$_8$ 9 significans] significat O   10 ita] sic O   11 materialiter] materia O   12 demonstrarentur] demonstratur E$_4$ E$_8$ || ipsa significata] ipsa significativa E$_4$ *inv.* O   13 determinari] demorari O || foret] esset O   15 pronominis] propositionis O || dicto] dicendo O   16 verum] vox O   18 verum] vox O   19 huius] *om.* O || ponatur] hoc O || suum significatum] *inv.* E$_4$ || sic] sicut E$_8$ est O   20 Hoc ... verum] verum est falsum O || Hoc] est falsum *add.* E$_8$ O || verum^2] et loco huius pronominis ponatur suum significatum sic: hoc est falsum est verum est falsum *add.* E$_4$ 21 terminaretur] terminetur E$_4$ || intellectus] intentio O || continue terminus] ex illo casu (*dub.*) E$_4$ 22 esset] et E$_4$ || alterius] unius E$_4$ E$_8$ 23 dicitur] potest dici O || licet] *om.* E$_4$ 23–24 possit] posset E$_4$ E$_8$ 24 absolute] et *add.* E$_8$ || neque^2] nec O   26 acceptum] accepta E$_4$ E$_8$ || denotare] demonstrare O   27 ideo] non E$_8$ vero O || supponat] supponit O || sic] simile O

significatively can be referred to even if ⟨this way of taking it⟩ may not be referred to by saying 'taken significatively'. Thus speaking in this way:

This is a sound,

referring ⟨by 'this'⟩ to the sound 'man', if it may indeed be referred to taken materially, I say that it may be referred to taken significatively even if it is not referred to under the intention 'taken significatively'. For it is the same to say:

This sound,

and:

This sound signifying a rational animal,

and so it is in the present case ⟨sc. of 'this' in A referring to B⟩. For in no way can there be a reciprocal reference unless they are referred to materially, because however else they may be referred to, the significates are referred to. And in such a case ⟨the hearer's⟩ comprehension could never be terminated regarding these significates, rather there would be an infinite ⟨referential⟩ circle always putting the significate of the ⟨demonstrative⟩ pronoun ⟨'this'⟩ in place of the pronoun, as manifestly appears in an utterance like ⟨A⟩:

This is true,

to say which it would be the same to say:

'This is false' is true,

and to put its significate in place of the pronoun, like this:

'"This is true" is false' is true.

And so the comprehension would never terminate, rather the term of the one would continually be ⟨replaced by⟩ the term of the other.[150]

ad 7.1.1.2–1 Alternatively, one might reply that although each utterance can be signified by the subject of the other utterance and is so absolutely, neither materially nor significatively, yet the subject of A does not supposit for B unless it is taken materially. For A cannot mean itself to be true of B taken significatively without contradiction and for that reason ⟨A's

---

[150] The threat of infinite regress described here is very similar to that described by John Dumbleton in his account of insolubles. See, e.g., Read, 'The Calculators and the Insolubles', pp. 147–48.

significative accepta, sed materialiter—et hoc posito quod alio modo non possit accipi nisi materialiter vel significative—sic ut significet A esse falsum. Et similiter subiectum ipsius B consimiliter restringitur ne supponat pro A sic significative accepta. Et secundum hoc facilis est responsio sicut patet intelligenti.

ad 7.1.1.2–2 Aliter dicitur ad hoc argumentum et probatur quod licet per hoc pronomen: hoc, possit indifferenter quodcumque singulariter signficari, non tamen sequitur quod pro quocumque possit supponere respectu cuiuscumque copule vel respectu cuiuscumque predicati, sicut iste terminus 'falsum', quodlibet falsum significat et non tamen quodlibet falsum supponit respectu cuiuscumque copule, ut superius patuit. Et secundum istum modum dicendi facilis est responsio. Hec enim est falsa:

Hoc est falsum,

et non quia denotat hoc predicatum in⟨esse⟩ A, sed quia est affirmativa et denotat predicatum inesse alicui pro quo subiectum supponit, cum tamen subiectum non supponat pro aliquo et ita denotat falsum sicut facit hoc:

Falsum dicitur a Sorte.

Et ita patet responsio ad hoc et ad omnia talia similia per que quidam nituntur probare quod universaliter pars potest supponere pro suo toto respectu cuiuscumque predicati vel copule, et hoc argumentum vocant achillem invictum cum tamen non deceat loripedem claudicantem militi tam strenuo comparare.

7.2 Alia sunt sophysmata que videntur | esse insolubilia et non sunt. E_8 33ra

7.2.1 Ut hoc: sit A nomen cuiuslibet negative respondentis in ista disputatione et proponatur:

Tu es A.

Si negatur, contra: tu negative respondes, ergo tu es A per casum. Si conceditur, contra: tu affirmative respondes in hac disputatione, ergo non es A.

---

1 alio modo non] non alio modo O 2 possit] posset E_4 E_8 ‖ materialiter vel significative] significative vel materialiter O 3 similiter] *om.* O ‖ restringitur] restringatur E_8 O ‖ ne] ut O ‖ supponat] supponunt E_4 4 accepta] accepit E_4 accepto O ‖ sicut] ut O 6 et probatur] probabile O ‖ licet] si E_4 7 possit] posset E_4 E_8 8 tamen sequitur] *inv.* O ‖ quod] *om.* E_4 ‖ possit] posse E_4 9 respectu²] *om.* O ‖ cuiuscumque²] *om.* E_8 O 10 et] *om.* O 10–11 quodlibet² falsum] pro quocumque falso O 11 copule] vel predicati *add.* O ‖ superius] prius E_4 12 enim] non E_8 14 denotat] denotatur E_8 denotet O 16 subiectum] suppositum E_4 ‖ supponat] supponit E_4 21 cuiuscumque] cuiusdam E_4 ‖ vel copule] *om.* O ‖ hoc] hanc E_4 22 achillem invictum] achilles invictus O ‖ tamen] videtur E_4 ‖ deceat] deiciat E_8 deiciant O ‖ loripedem] loyci pedem O 22–23 militi … comparare] unde immerito debet tam strenuo militi comparari E_4 unde merito debet tali strenuo militi comparari O 24 sophysmata] *om.* O ‖ esse] *om.* O 25 Ut] sicut O ‖ hoc] hoc *vel* hic (*dub.*) E_4 hec E_8 ‖ respondentis] responsive E_4 E_8 28 contra] extra E_4 29 in hac disputatione] *om.* O ‖ ergo] tu *add.* O

subject⟩ is restricted so that it does not supposit for B taken significatively, but materially—and this having assumed that it can only be taken materially or significatively—so that ⟨B⟩ signifies that A is false. And similarly, the subject of B is restricted likewise so that it does not supposit for A taken significatively. And according to that way of speaking the response is easy, as is clear to the one who understands it.[151]

ad 7.1.1.2–2 Another possibility is to reply to this argument by proving that although anything whatever could be indifferently signified singularly by the pronoun 'this', yet it does not follow that it could supposit for anything whatever, whatever the copula or whatever the predicate, just as the term 'falsehood' signifies any falsehood whatever and yet does not supposit for any falsehood whatever, whatever the copula, as is clear from the above ⟨chapters⟩. And according to this way of replying, the response is easy. For ⟨B⟩:

> This is false

is false and not because it means that this predicate ⟨'false'⟩ belongs to A, but because it is an affirmative and means that the predicate belongs to something for which the subject supposits while nonetheless the subject does not supposit for anything, and so it comes out false, just like:

> A falsehood is said by Socrates.[152]

And so the response is clear to this and to all similar arguments by means of which some people endeavour to prove that the part can supposit universally for its whole with respect to any predicate or copula whatever. They call this argument an "invincible Achilles",[153] when, however, it is not fitting to compare a club-footed cripple to such a vigorous soldier.

7.2 There are other sophisms which seem to be but are not insolubles.

7.2.1 Like this: let A be the name of anyone responding negatively in this disputation and let:

> You are an A

be proposed. If you deny it, on the contrary: you respond negatively, therefore you are an A by the scenario. If you grant it, on the contrary: you respond affirmatively in this disputation, therefore you are not an A.[154]

---

[151] Segrave seems here to take §7.1.1 to be an insoluble and so to be solved by his restrictivist account.

[152] See §6.3.3 above. So perhaps Segrave thinks the example in §7.1.1 is an insoluble after all, and to be solved by the fallacy of accident.

[153] One of these people was Bradwardine: see his *Insolubilia*, §4.2.3 and §ad 4.2.3 (p. 168).

[154] Cf. Bradwardine, *Insolubilia*, §11.2. According to Pozzi, *Il Mentitore e il Medioevo*, p. 361, n. 266, this sophism is found also in Buridan, Marsilius of Inghen and Henry Hopton. However, in Buridan's *Summulae* the sophism occurs in the explicit form 'You will respond negatively' (Buridan, *Summulae*, tr. Klima, p. 991, sophism 16; ed. Pironet, p. 179: *tu respondebis negative*). There is a sophism more similar to Segrave's 7.2.1 in Marsilius' *Insolubilia*, in the discussion of the fourth sophism in ch. 3 (ms Pal.lat. 995, f. 72v): "Sic solvitur hoc sophisma similiter: ponatur a significat omne negative responsurum et nullum alium et quod numquam respondebis nisi una responsione quam primo michi facies ad proposi-

7.2.2 Simile est: sit A nomen cuiuslibet aliter respondentis quam affirmative.

7.2.3 Simile est: proponatur hec:

Tu negative respondes in A,

sit A tempus in quo respondebis ad hanc [vel] ⟨et⟩ ad nullam aliam. Si conceditur, concedis falsum pro tempore pro quo est falsum, ergo male respondes. Si negetur, negetur verum pro tempore pro quo est verum etc.

ad 7.2.1–7.2.3 Ad ista et similia que capiunt veritatem vel falsitatem ex modo respondendi, modo respondendum est uno modo negando actum propositum quia ex responsione negativa fiunt vera et ex affirmativa fiunt falsa.

ad 7.2.1 Et ideo cum proponitur hec:

Tu es A,

neganda est, et cum arguitur:

Tu negative respondes ad istam ⟨ergo tu es A⟩,

neganda est non quia falsa, sed quia repugnans casui. Ex hac enim et casu sequitur unum quod in omni casu negandum est tamquam falsum si non fiat obligatio in contrarium. Sequitur enim:

Omnis negative respondens est A, tu negative respondes
ad istam, ergo tu es A,

ergo male respondes quia negas verum non obligatus. Istud debet semper defendi tamquam repugnans, et consequentia patet quia non sumus in casu ubi accidit insolubile cum nec ponatur hic verum nec falsum nec equivalens.

7.2.1.1 Sed dices postquam: tales propositiones veritatem contrahunt si negentur, et falsitatem si concedantur; quare non debeo illas concedere et negare actum propositum ita bene | sicut negare illas.

---

1 est] si *add.* O || aliter respondentis] *inv.* O   4 A] et *add.* O   5 respondebis] respondes O || hanc] illam O   6 conceditur] concedis O || pro^2] *om.* O || ergo] tu *add.* O   7 negetur, negetur] negis negis O negatur E$_4$ || pro^2] *om.* O   8 et] ad *add.* E$_4$ || vel] et E$_4$ 9 modo respondendum est uno modo] est uno modo respondendum O   10 ex^2] responsione O   14–16 et ... est] *om. hom.* E$_8$ 17 est] *om.* E$_4$ 18 fiat] *om.* O   19 Omnis negative] aliquis negare O || est] ad *add.* O   20 ergo] *om.* E$_4$ E$_8$ 21 obligatus] et O   21–22 debet ... defendi] semper defendi debet O   21 debet semper] *inv.* E$_4$ 22 et] *om.* E$_4$ 23 ubi] nisi O || ponatur hic] ponitur nec O   25 tales] iste O   26 negentur] negantur E$_4$ O || et^1] *om.* O || debeo] concedis O

7.2.2 A similar one: let A be the name of anyone responding otherwise than affirmatively.[155]

7.2.3 A similar one: let this be proposed:

> You respond negatively at A,

where A is the time at which you will respond to this proposition and to no other. If you grant it, you grant a falsehood at the time at which it is a falsehood, therefore you respond wrongly. If you deny it, you deny a truth at the time at which it is a truth, ⟨therefore you respond wrongly⟩.

ad 7.2.1–7.2.3 To these and similar sophisms which derive truth or falsehood from the way of responding, one should respond in one way, ⟨viz⟩ by denying that response because from a negative response they become true and from an affirmative they become false.

ad 7.2.1 For that reason when this proposition:

> You are an A,

is proposed, it should be denied, and when it is argued:

> You respond negatively to this, ⟨so you are an A⟩,

this should be denied not because it is false, but because it is inconsistent with the scenario. For from this proposition together with the scenario, one conclusion should be denied in every scenario as false if no obligation to the contrary is set up ⟨e.g. that you should respond affirmatively⟩. For this inference is valid:

> Everyone responding negatively is an A, you respond negatively to this, therefore you are an A,

therefore you respond badly because you deny a truth while under no obligation ⟨to do so⟩. That conclusion should always be rejected as inconsistent, and the inference is clear because we are not in a scenario where an insoluble results since here neither 'truth' nor 'falsehood' nor an equivalent[156] term occurs.

7.2.1.1 But you may reply: these propositions become infected with truth if they are denied, and with falsehood if they are granted. Why should I not grant them and deny that response just as well as deny them?

---

tionem quam tibi proponam et tunc propositio i(s)ta est: tu non es a. Manifestum est enim quod in hoc casu idem est querere tu es a et tu es michi responsurus." As for Hopton, the attribution of the treatise in question is questionable, and in any case the text is merely an adaptation of Bradwardine's treatise (see Bradwardine, *Insolubilia*, 'Introduction' p. 38): the sophism is found on ff. 18vb–19ra of the manuscript.

[155] See, e.g., Pironet, *Guillaume Heytesbury: Sophismata Asinina*, sophism 34 (pp. 327, 431, 481) and Synan, 'The *Insolubilia* of Roger Nottingham, O.F.M.', p. 270, §63; in §64 he replies that the proposition 'Tu es A' ('You are an A') should be doubted.

[156] See §6.13.1.

ad 7.2.1.1 Et dico quod causa est quia licet homo possit ita respondere, magis tamen inconveniens sequitur: qui concedit, ipse ponit quod significatur per concessum. Unde qui concedit se esse A, ponit se negative respondere, sed qui negat, nihil ponit. Ideo minus inconveniens accidit hic quam ibi.

ad 7.2–7.2.3 Aliter dicitur et bene quod ad tales propositiones, que veritatem capiunt ex hoc quod negantur a respondente et falsitatem ex hoc quod conceduntur, non est respondendum pro tempore quo dependent ex actu respondendi sed pro alio tempore quo non dependent.

ad 7.2.3 Ut si proponatur hec:

Tu negative respondes,

ad istam non est respondendum pro tempore quo respondeo, sed pro alio tempore quia si respondeam pro illo tempore responsionis mee vel oportet negare verum pro tempore quo est verum vel concedere falsum pro tempore quo est falsum. Et ratio istius positionis est hec: quia veritas istius responsionis debet dependere ex veritate vel falsitate illius ad quod respondetur et non e contra, ymmo veritas illius ad quod respondetur presupponitur naturaliter ante realem concessionem istius et hoc pro tempore pro quo conceditur, etsi non in tempore in quo conceditur. Et secundum istum modum | patet responsio ad omnia talia satis facilis.   O 3rb

aliter ad 7.2.1–7.2.3 Aliter ad hec dicitur quod huiusmodi institutiones dependentes ut sic:

A ⟨est⟩ nomen cuiuslibet negative respondentis etc.

non sunt admittende nisi sub conditione quod non proponatur aliquod tale contrahens veritatem ex actu negandi nec falsitatem ex actu concedendi, sicut nec sunt huiusmodi institutiones admittende nisi sub conditione ut convertatur A cum isto termino: asinus in propositione vera et cum isto termino: homo in propositione falsa, | ista institutio non est admittenda   E₈ 33va

---

1 Et] *om.* E₄ ‖ quia] *om.* E₄ ‖ possit] posset E₄ E₈ ‖ ita] bene *add.* O   2 qui] quia E₄ *om.* O ‖ ponit] ponatur E₄   3 Unde qui concedit] unum quem concedere O   4 Ideo] ergo O ‖ accidit] est et sequatur O   9 ex] in *add.* E₄ ‖ respondendi] *om.* E₄   10 proponatur] proponitur   12 ad ... respondendum] *om.* O ‖ pro¹] illo O ‖ tempore] pro *add.* E₄ ‖ respondeo] est responsio O   13 si] *non scr. et del.* O ‖ responsionis mee] respondeo negative O   14 oportet] oporteret E₈   15 tempore] pro *add.* E₄ ‖ istius] huius O   15–16 est ... responsionis] est hec quia veritas responsionis *add. mss*   16 vel falsitate] vel falsitatem E₄ *om.* O   17 et non ... respondetur] *om. hom.* O   18 realem] *lacuna in* E₈   19 pro] *om.* O   20 facilis] facilia E₄ faciliter O   21 huiusmodi] huius E₄ hee O   26 nec] *om.* O ‖ huiusmodi] huius E₄ ‖ nisi] nec O   28 ista institutio] institutio hac E₄ ‖ non] *om.* E₄

ad 7.2.1.1 I reply that the reason is that, although a man can respond in this way, nonetheless a greater inconvenience ensues: one who grants anything affirms what is signified by what was granted. For that reason one who grants that he is an A claims that he responds negatively; but one who denies something, does not affirm anything. So a lesser inconvenience results from ⟨my response⟩ than from the other.

ad 7.2–7.2.3 Alternatively, one might reply, and correctly, that the response to these propositions, which become true from being denied by the respondent and become false from being granted, should not be given for a time at which the propositions depend on the act of responding, but for another time at which they are not dependent.

ad 7.2.3 E.g., if this:

You respond negatively

is proposed, the response to it should not be given for the time at which I respond, but for another time, because if my response is given for the time of my response, either it is necessary to deny a truth for the time at which it is a truth or to grant a falsehood for the time at which it is a falsehood.[157] And the reason for this solution is this: because the truth of this response ⟨sc. to 'You respond negatively'⟩ should depend on the truth or falsity of that to which it is a response and not conversely; indeed, the truth of that to which it is a response is naturally presupposed before its actual granting, and this for the time for which it is granted, although not at the time at which it is granted. And according to this way of replying, it is clear that the response to all these sophisms is quite easy.

aliter ad 7.2.1–7.2.3 Alternatively, one might reply to these sophisms that this kind of dependent imposition,[158] like:

A ⟨is⟩ the name of anyone responding negatively etc.,

should only be admitted on the condition that nothing is proposed which becomes true from an act of denying or becomes false from an act of granting. So impositions of this kind should only be admitted on condition, e.g., the imposition that A converts with the term 'ass' in a true proposition and with the term 'man' in a false proposition[159] should only

---

[157] Cf. Burley, *Obligations*, tr. Kretzmann and Stump, §3.73.
[158] On dependent imposition (institutio dependens) see Burley, *De obligationibus*, ed. Green, §§1.14–1.22 (vol. II, pp. 37–38): "Dependent imposition is that which depends on an act of use [...] One rule given for dependent imposition is this: Dependent imposition should only be admitted on condition" (Institutio dependens est quae dependet ab actu utentis [...] de institutione dependenti talis datur regula: institutio dependens non est admittenda nisi sub conditione). (N.B. the section of Burley's text on dependent imposition is omitted from Kretzmann and Stump's translation.)
[159] This is an example of *institutio absoluta*: see, for example, Burley, *De obligationibus*, ed. Green, §§1.02–1.03, p. 35 (tr. Kretzmann and Stump, p. 371).

nisi sub hac conditione quod non coniugatur cum aliquo termino tali ubi sequitur, si tota propositio sit vera, quod sit falsa, ut hec:

 Tu es A,

vel:

 Homo est A,

vel:

 Asinus est A

sequitur enim:

 Hec est vera: Homo est A, ergo A convertitur cum isto termino: asinus, ergo est falsa.

Et sic patet ad talia.

7.3 Aliter paralogizatur sic: Multa sunt entia nomina non habentia, et hoc loquendo de nomine positivo; non enim est aliquid quin habeat vel nomen positivum vel privativum quia quodlibet est nominatum vel innominatum. Tunc possibile est A esse nomen cuiuslibet innominati. Ponatur ergo inesse et demonstro aliquod tale; hec est vera:

 Hoc est A

Et sequitur ultra: ergo est innominatum, per casum. Consequens tamen falsum quia A est nomen eius.

7.3.1 Simile est posito quod Sortes non habeat nunc nisi hoc nomen: Sortes. Possibile est A | imponi cuilibet non habenti duo nomina. Ponatur ergo inesse; vel ergo Sortes est A vel non, et patet deductio.

ad 7.3 Ad ista dico quod hec est distinguenda:

 possibile est A esse nomen cuiuslibet innominati

secundum divisionem et compositionem. In sensu composito est falsa, est enim sensus:

 Hec est possibilis: A est nomen cuiuslibet innominati,

et hoc loquendo de nomine positivo, et hoc est falsum. Sensus divisus est verus et est sensus:

---

2 sequitur] quod *add.* O 5 est] omnis (*dub.*) *add.* E$_4$ 6 vel] *om.* E$_4$ E$_8$ 7 est] *om.* E$_4$ 8 enim] *om.* E$_4$ 9 Homo] hoc E$_4$ O || est A] *om.* O || A^2] *om.* O ibi *vel* vel (*dub.*) *add.* E$_4$ 12 Aliter] sic *add.* E$_4$ 13 non enim] quia non O || aliquid] aliquod E$_4$ || quin] quod non O 14 vel nomen] *inv.* E$_4$ || vel^2] nomen *add.* O || quodlibet] vel *add.* O 15 A esse] *inv.* O 16 Ponatur ergo] *iter.* O || hec] hoc E$_4$ 17 Hoc] hec E$_4$ 18 per casum] *om.* O || tamen] est *add.* O 20 est] enim O || nisi] unicum *add.* E$_4$ || hoc] istud O 22 ergo^2] *om.* O 23 hec est distinguenda] distinguenda est hec O 25 divisionem et compositionem] compositionem et divisionem O || composito] et E$_4$ 26 est enim] et est E$_4$ 27 Hec est possibilis] *om.* O || est possibilis ... nomen] est nomen A est possibilis E$_4$ 28 divisus] divisionis E$_4$ 29 verus] verum E$_8$ O

be admitted on the condition that it is not conjoined with any term where it follows that if the whole proposition is true, it is false; e.g.,

>You are an A,

or

>A man is an A,

or

>An ass is an A,

for this inference is valid:

>'A man is an A' is true, therefore A converts with the term 'ass', therefore ⟨'A man is an A'⟩ is false.

And so the response to such sophisms is clear.

7.3 A paralogism can be made in another way like this: There are many beings which do not have names, speaking here of positive names; for there isn't anything which does not have a name, either positive or privative, because everything is named or unnamed. Then it is possible that A is a name of everything which is unnamed. So suppose that ⟨A⟩ applies ⟨to everything unnamed⟩ and I refer to such a thing. ⟨So⟩ this is true:

>This is A,

and then by the scenario it follows that it is unnamed. Yet the conclusion is false because A is a name of it.[160]

7.3.1 It is similar supposing that Socrates now has only this name 'Socrates'. ⟨Then⟩ it is possible that A is imposed on everything not having two names. So suppose that ⟨A⟩ applies ⟨to everything not having two names⟩; so either Socrates is A or not. And the argument is clear.[161]

ad 7.3 I reply to these sophisms that:

>It is possible that A is the name of everything unnamed

should be disambiguated according to the divided and composite senses. In the composite sense it is false, for the sense is:

>This is possible: A is the name of everything unnamed,

and speaking of a positive name, this is false. The divided sense is true and the sense is:

---

[160] Cf. Bradwardine, *Insolubilia*, §11.4.
[161] Cf. Bradwardine, *Insolubilia*, §11.3.

Cuiuslibet nunc innominati possibile est ut A sit nomen, sicut illud quod nunc est album possibile est ut sit nigrum, tamen hoc non est possibile album esse nigrum.

ad 7.3.1 Et eadem est responsio ad similia.

7.4 Alia sunt sophysmata que videntur esse insolubilia et non sunt, ut:

Equivocum est univocum.

ad 7.4 Et illa | similiter solvenda sunt per distinctionem. Subiectum enim propositionis respectu predicati secunde impositionis potest habere suppositionem simplicem vel personalem. Si simplicem, vera est et est sensus:

Hoc nomen equivocum est univocum,

et hec est vera quia significat omnia sua significata per unum nomen et unam rationem. Diffinitio enim huius nominis: equivocum competit omnibus equivocis secundum quod sunt equivoca. Si autem habeat suppositionem personalem, falsa est et est sensus:

Aliquod suppositum huius termini: equivocum est univocum,

sicut canis et consimilia, et hoc est falsum.

7.5 Alia sunt sophysmata que ortum habent ex actu voluntatis et ista sunt difficiliora aliis.

---

1 nunc] *om.* O ‖ ut] quod O ‖ nomen] et *add.* O   2 sicut] quod E$_8$ est *add.* O ‖ illud] *om.* O ‖ est^2] *om.* E$_8$ ‖ ut sit] esse O ‖ tamen hoc] et re (*dub.*) ex hoc E$_4$ 3 esse] est O   4 est responsio] *inv.* O   5 esse] *om.* E$_4$ O ‖ ut] *om.* E$_4$ 6 est univocum] cum univoco E$_8$ 7 Et] *om.* O ‖ similiter] similia E$_4$ ‖ solvenda] dissolvenda E$_8$ 9–10 est sensus] *inv.* O   11 equivocum ... univocum] est equivocum E$_4$ 12 hec] hoc O ‖ est vera quia] vera O   13 et] per *add.* E$_4$ ‖ equivocum] *iter.* E$_4$ 14 omnibus equivocis] *inv.* O ‖ habeat] habeant O   16 est] si O   18 consimilia] similia E$_4$ talia O   19 et ista sunt] *om.* E$_4$ E$_8$

Of anything now unnamed, it is possible that A be a name of it,

just as of what is now white it is possible that it be black; however, it is not possible that what is white is black.

ad 7.3.1 And the response is the same to the similar sophisms.

7.4 There are other sophisms which seem to be but are not insolubles, e.g.,

⟨An⟩ equivocal is univocal.[162]

ad 7.4 These sophisms should similarly be solved by means of a disambiguation. For the subject of a proposition can have simple or personal supposition with respect to a predicate of second imposition.[163] If ⟨the subject has⟩ simple ⟨supposition, the proposition 'Equivocal is univocal'⟩ is true and the sense is:

This name 'equivocal' is univocal,

and this is true because it signifies all its significates by means of one name and one essential definition.[164] For the definition of the name 'equivocal' is applicable to all equivocals insofar as they are equivocals. But if ⟨the subject⟩ has personal supposition, then ⟨'⟨An⟩ equivocal is univocal'⟩ is false and the sense is:

Some suppositum of the term 'equivocal' is univocal,

like 'dog' and similar terms, and this is false.[165]

7.5 There are other sophisms which derive from an act of will and they are more difficult than the others.[166]

---

[162] Cf. Bradwardine, *Insolubilia*, §11.1.
[163] On first and second imposition, see, e.g., Ockham, *Summa Logicae*, I 11. For this rule, see the first rule of equivocation, *ibid.*, III-4 ch. 4.
[164] See Aristotle, *Categories*, ch. 1.
[165] Cf. Bradwardine, *Insolubilia*, §ad 11.1.1.
[166] Some sophisms on acts of will, but not those presented by Segrave, are found in Kilvington's *Questions on Aristotle's Ethics*, ed. Michalowska, p. 153 ff. The fourth sophism in Marsilius' *Insolubilia* reads: "The fourth sophism is like this: suppose that Socrates wants to eat if Plato wants to eat and otherwise not. Then it is asked whether Socrates want to eat. And if so, then Plato wants to eat, ⟨and⟩ furthermore, then Socrates does not want to eat. If it is said that ⟨Socrates⟩ does not ⟨want to eat⟩, then Plato wants to eat and furthermore, then Socrates wants to eat. Hence from first to last, if Socrates does not want to eat Socrates does want to eat" (Quartum sophisma sit tale: ponamus quod sortes volt comedere si plato volt comedere et aliter non est, et quod econtra plato volt comedere si sortes non volt comedere et aliter non est. Tunc queritur [utrum etc] utrum sortes volt comedere. Et si sic ergo plato volt comedere. Ultra ergo sortes non volt comedere. Si dicitur quod non, ergo plato volt comedere et ultra ergo sortes volt comedere, ergo de primo ad ultimum, si sortes non volt comedere sortes volt comedere). (Pal.lat. 995, f. 86r.) He adds (f. 86v): "Another sophism: Socrates wants to run if Plato wants to run and not otherwise, and Plato wants to run if Socrates does not want to run" (Aliud sophisma: sortes volt currere si plato volt currere et non aliter, et plato volt currere si sortes non volt currere), but doesn't elaborate. The sophism 'Socrates vult comedere' is also found in Buridan, *Sophismata* (ed.Pironet, p. 183). The sophism 'quod Sortes velit currere si Plato velit currere et aliter non, et quod Plato velit

7.5.1 Ut hoc posito quod Sortes velit aliquid, puta A—sit A aliquis effectus volubilis—sub ista conditione quod Plato velit illud et non aliter et quod Plato velit A sub ista conditione quod Sortes non velit illud. Iste casus patet per hoc quod voluntas est respectu impossibilium, ergo quilibet potest conditionare volitum per quamcumque conditionem sibi placuerit. Quero utrum Sortes vult A vel non. Si vult, ergo Plato vult per casum, et sequitur: Plato vult, ergo Sortes non vult per aliam partem casus, ergo ⟨Sortes non vult A⟩. Si non vult Sortes, ergo Plato vult per casum, et sequitur ultra: ergo Sortes vult, quia sub illa conditione vult Sortes, ergo posita conditione, ponitur ipsum velle.

7.5.2 Similiter: velit Sortes malum omnibus volentibus sibi malum et Plato e contra omnibus non volentibus sibi malum; aut | ergo vult Sortes Platoni malum vel non; et patet deductio.

7.5.3 Simile est: Maledicat Sortes omnibus maledicentibus sibi sic dicendo:
    Maledicantur omnes mihi maledicentes,
et Plato e contra sic dicendo:
    Maledicantur omnes mihi non maledicentes.
Aut ergo maledicit Sortes Platoni aut non; et patet deductio sicut in aliis.

ad 7.5.1 Ad primum dico quod hec est distinguenda:
    Sortes vult A sub hac conditione quod Plato velit A,
et similiter alia pars casus ex eo quod potest esse conditionalis vel de conditionato extremo. Si utraque sit conditionalis, repugnat, sicut probat

---

2 Plato] Petrus *passim* O ‖ et non aliter] *om.* O   3 A] istum O   4 per hoc quod] quia O ‖ impossibilium] possibilium O   5 volitum ... conditionem] voluntatem sub quacumque conditione O ‖ sibi] ubi E$_4$ ‖ placuerit] placuit O   6 vult^1] velit O ‖ Si] Sortes *add.* O ‖ Plato vult] *inv.* E$_4$ 8 Sortes ... A] etc. *mss*   9 ergo^1] *om.* E$_4$ 11 Similiter] simile O ‖ velit] est velud E$_4$ ‖ malum^2] *om.* O   12 contra] converso O ‖ aut ergo] *inv.* E$_4$ 13 vel] et O   15 omnes] communes O   15–17 maledicentes ... mihi] *om. hom.* E$_4$ 16–17 et Plato ... maledicentes] *om. hom.* O   18 aut] vel E$_4$ ‖ sicut] et *add.* O   19 hec] ista O   20 quod] qua O ‖ velit] vult O ‖ A^2] *om.* E$_4$ E$_8$

7.5.1 For example, suppose that Socrates wills something, e.g. A—where A is some willable object—on the condition that Plato wills ⟨A⟩ and not otherwise and that Plato wills A on the condition that Socrates does not will ⟨A⟩. The scenario is clear by the fact that the will embraces impossible things,[167] therefore anyone can impose any condition whatever on what is willed that pleases him. I ask if Socrates wills A or not. If he wills ⟨A⟩, then according to the scenario Plato wills ⟨A⟩ so it follows that Plato wills ⟨A⟩, whence according to the other part of the scenario Socrates does not will ⟨A⟩, and so ⟨Socrates does not will A⟩. If Socrates does not will ⟨A⟩, then according to the scenario Plato wills ⟨A⟩ so it follows that Socrates wills ⟨A⟩, because Socrates wills ⟨A⟩ on the condition ⟨that Plato wills A⟩. Therefore, when the condition is satisfied, his willing ⟨A⟩ ensues.

7.5.2 Similarly: let Socrates will bad things for everyone who wills bad things for ⟨Socrates⟩ himself and conversely let Plato will bad things for everyone who does not will bad things for ⟨Plato⟩ himself.[168] So either Socrates wills bad things for Plato or not; and the argument is clear.

7.5.3 It is similar supposing that Socrates bad-mouths everyone who bad-mouths him by uttering this:

> Everyone who bad-mouths me should be bad-mouthed,

and Plato does the converse by uttering this:

> Everyone who does not bad-mouth me should be bad-mouthed.[169]

Then either Socrates bad-mouths Plato or not; and the argument is clear as in the other cases.

ad 7.5.1 To the first I say that this:

> Socrates wills A under the condition that Plato wills A,

should be disambiguated, and the other part of the scenario similarly, because it can be a conditional proposition or one having a conditioned extreme.[170] If each is a conditional proposition, then they are inconsistent

---

currere si Sortes non velit currere et aliter non' occurs in Roger Roseth: see Murdoch, 'From Social into Intellectual Factors', in *The Cultural Context of Medieval Learning*, p. 325 n. 95.

[167] Cf. Aristotle, *Nicomachean Ethics*, III.5, 1111b22 ("Voluntas autem est inpossiblium, puta inmortalitatis") in Aristotle, *Ethica Nicomachea*, ed. Gautier, p. 414, 16.17.

[168] The sophism 'Socrates wishes Plato evil' (*Socrates optat malum Platoni*) is found in Buridan's *Sophismata*, tr. Klima, p. 996, ed. Pironet, p. 185.

[169] This sophism is found in Buridan's *Sophismata* (tr. Klima, p. 995, ed. Pironet, p. 184).

[170] See, e.g., Paul of Venice, *Logica Magna: De Conditionali*, ed. and tr. Hughes, §1, pp. 2–6. It marks a scope distinction: taken as having a conditioned extreme, 'Socrates wills A on the condition that Plato wills A' reads: 'Socrates wills ⟨A on the condition that Plato wills A⟩', that is 'Socrates wills, on the condition that Plato wills A, A'; taken as a conditional, it reads: 'On the condition that Plato wills A, Socrates wills A', that is, 'If Plato wills A, Socrates wills A'.

argumentum. Si de conditionatis extremis, sic est casus possibilis et tunc est sensus:

> Sortes vult A sic conditionatum quod Plato velit illud ita esse quod voluntas Sortis feratur non in A absolute, sed in A sic conditionato,

sicut ego volo esse in luto cum centum marcis, et tamen ⟨non⟩ volo esse in luto.

Hoc posito dico quod neuter vult A, sed uterque vult A cum conditione vel conditionatim et sic numquam erit argumentum, quia ex illis de conditionatis extremis non sequuntur | ille conditionales. Non enim sequitur ex Sortem velle esse in luto cum centum marcis, ipsum velle esse in luto et quecumque conditio ponatur inesse.

O 3va

ad 7.5.2 Ad alia similiter est respondendum, unde qui habet voluntatem respectu alicuius universalis vel sub intentione universali solum, non habet voluntatem respectu alicuius particularis nisi conditionaliter, videlicet si ipsum contineatur sub illo | universali. Unde voluntas generalis non est voluntas respectu particularis nisi conditionata. Hoc posito neuter vult alteri malum simpliciter sed uterque vult malum conditionaliter, puta si ipsum contineatur sub illo generali in quod fertur sua voluntas.

E$_8$ 34rb

ad 7.5.3 Pro tertio sciendum quod maledicere non solum est dicere malum, sed dicere malum in predicando illud alicui cum voluntate ut illud sibi accidat. Unde neuter istorum vult malum alteri simpliciter, sed conditionaliter et secundum quid sicut nec in alio casu. Unde neuter malum dicit alteri nec alicui simpliciter, sed conditionaliter, puta si ille sit maledicens mihi vel si ille sit mihi non maledicens. Unde si non exprimatur illa conditio, tacite tamen intelligitur in illo generali, ergo etc.

Expliciunt insolubilia Magistri Walteri de Sexgrave de Anglia Amen.

---

3 sic] ita O ‖ conditionatum] conditionatim E$_8$ conditionatus O   4 non] *om.* E$_8$ O ‖ absolute] *add. in marg.* E$_4$ 6 marcis] mortis E$_8$ ducatis O ‖ et tamen] ergo ego O   8 dico] *om.* O ‖ uterque] utrumque E$_8$ O   9 conditionatim] conditionatus O ‖ quia] *om.* E$_8$ ‖ de] *om.* O   10 enim] *om.* E$_4$ 11 ex Sortem velle] ex eo quod Sortes velit O ‖ marcis] mortis E$_8$ ducatis O ‖ ipsum velle] quod ipse velit O   13 voluntatem] *om.* O   14 universalis] talis O   15 respectu] *om.* O ‖ conditionaliter] conditionatus conditio autem O ‖ videlicet] valet O   17 respectu] *om.* O   18 malum^2] *om.* E$_4$ 19 sub] in O ‖ fertur] ferretur E$_4$ E$_8$ 20 tertio] est *add.* O ‖ maledicere] malum dicere E$_4$ 21 illud^2] aliud E$_8$ animo O   22 malum alteri] *inv.* O   23 neuter] istorum *add.* O   23–24 malum dicit alteri] maledicit O   24 conditionaliter] ut *add.* O   25 vel] sibi ulterius *add.* O ‖ mihi ... maledicens] *om. hom.* E$_4$ 26 tamen] *om.* O ‖ illo] illa O ‖ etc] Stude Antoni quia proderit tibi multum *add.* O   27 Expliciunt ... Amen] Magister Walterii de Sexgrave de Anglia etc. E$_8$ ‖ Walteri] Gualteri O ‖ de Sexgrave] *lac.* E$_4$ ‖ de Anglia Amen] cuius anima requiescat in pace, completa per me Antonium de Monte. M° III^c lxxxxv° die veneris quintodecimo mensis octobris post botos immediate O

with each other, as the argument shows.[171] If each has a conditioned extreme, in this way the scenario is possible and then the sense is:

> Socrates wills A so conditioned that Plato wills it so to be that Socrates' will is not directed towards A without qualification, but towards A conditioned in that way,

just as I will my being covered with mud for one hundred marks[172], but I do ⟨not⟩ will my being covered with mud ⟨without qualification⟩.[173]

Having stated that, I reply that neither ⟨Socrates nor Plato⟩ wills A ⟨without qualification⟩, but each wills A on a condition, that is, in a conditioned way,[174] and in this way the argument will never work, because from these propositions with conditioned extremes those conditional propositions do not follow. For from Socrates willing his being covered with mud for one hundred marks it does not follow that he wills his being covered with mud regardless of any condition imposed.

ad 7.5.2 One should respond to the other sophisms similarly, because anyone who has a will in respect of a universal object or one contained only under a universal intention, only has a will on a condition in respect of something partial, namely if that object is contained under that universal object. For that reason a general will is only a will in respect of something partial if the will is conditioned ⟨in some way⟩. On that assumption, neither ⟨Socrates nor Plato⟩ wills bad things for the other without qualification, but each wills bad things on a condition, e.g. if it is contained under that general object towards which his will is directed.

ad 7.5.3 With regard to the third argument, recall that to bad-mouth is not only to say bad things, but to say bad things predicating them of someone while willing bad things to befall him. So neither of them wills bad things for the other unconditionally, but on a condition and subject to a qualification, just as in the first case ⟨§ad 7.5.1⟩. For neither ⟨Socrates nor Plato⟩ bad-mouths the other nor anyone without qualification, but on a condition, e.g. if he is bad-mouthing me or if he is not bad-mouthing me. Thus if the condition is not overtly expressed, nonetheless it ⟨should be⟩ tacitly understood in the general object, therefore ⟨it is not without qualification, but conditional⟩.

Here end the insolubles of Master Walter of Segrave, from England.

---

[171] In §7.5.1, the paradox is clearly elaborated by a sequence of conditionals.
[172] A mark was two-thirds of a pound, that is, 13 shillings and fourpence. A hundred marks was a lot of money.
[173] The example is found in Burley, *De Puritate*, ed. Boehner, p. 87; tr. Spade, p. 175: see Read, 'Inferences', pp. 183–84.
[174] The adverb 'conditionatim' is not listed in Latham et al. (eds), *Dictionary of Medieval Latin from British Sources*, but is constructed in the same way as the adverbs 'copulatim' and disiunctim' (whose logical use is not recorded in the *Dictionary* either). All three expressions are found in, e.g., Maulfelt's *De suppositionibus* (see Read, *'Descensus copulatim*: Albert of Saxony and Thomas Maulfelt', p. 74).

Bibliography

Aquinas, *In III Sententiarum*, ed. Centre Traditio Litterarum Occidentalium (Turnhout: Brepols, 2010).

Aristotle, *De Interpretatione*, Latin tr. A. M. S. Boethius, in Aristoteles, *De Interpretatione vel Periermenias: Translatio Boethii, Specimina translationum recentiorum*, ed. L. Minio-Paluello. *Translatio Guillelmi de Moerbeka*, ed. Gerardus Verbeke, Aristoteles Latinus II 1–2 (Bruges: Desclée de Brouwer, 1965).

Aristotle, *De Sophisticis Elenchis*, in Aristoteles, *De Sophisticis Elenchis: Translatio Boethii, Fragmenta Translationis Iacobi et Recensio Guillelmi de Moerbeke*, ed. Bernardus G. Dod, Aristoteles Latinus VI 1–3 (Turnhout: Brepols, 1975).

Aristotle, *Ethica Nicomachea*, in Aristoteles, *Ethica Nicomachea : translatio Roberti Grosseteste Lincolniensis sive "Liber ethicorum", B. recensio recognita*, ed. Renatus Antonius Gauthier, Aristoteles Latinus, XXVI 1–3 (Leiden: Brill; Brussels: Desclée de Brouwer, 1973).

Aristotle, *Metaphysica*, in Aristoteles, *Metaphysica: Recensio Guillelmi de Moerbeke*, ed. Gudrun Vuillemin-Diem, Aristoteles Latinus XXV 3 (Leiden: Brill, 1995).

Aristotle, *Metaphysics*, Eng. tr. Richard Hope (Ann Arbor: University of Michigan Press, 1952).

Aristotle, *On the Soul (De Anima)*, Books II and III, Eng. tr. D. W. Hamlyn (Oxford: Clarendon Press, 1968).

Aristotle, *Posterior Analytics*, Eng. tr. with a commentary by Jonathan Barnes (Oxford: Clarendon Press, 1994).

Aristotle, *Prior Analytics: Book I*, Eng. tr. with an introduction and commentary by Gisela Striker (Oxford: Clarendon Press, 2009).

Aristotle, *Sophistical Refutations (De Sophisticis Elenchis)*, Eng. tr. Arthur W. Pickard-Cambridge, in *The Works of Aristotle*, ed. W. D. Ross, vol. I (Oxford: Oxford University Press, 1928), https://doi.org/10.1515/9781400835843-009.

Ashworth, E. J., *Logic and Language in the Post-Medieval Period*, Synthese Historical Library vol. 12 (Dordrecht: Springer, 1974), https://doi.org/10.1007/978-94-010-2226-2.

Augustine, *De Mendacio*, ed. J. Zycha (Turnhout: Brepols, 2010).

Averroes, *Aristotelis Metaphysicorum libri XIIII cum Averrois Cordubensis in eosdem Commentariis*, in *Aristotelis opera cum Averrois commentariis*, vol. VIII (Venice: apud Junctas, 1562), https://archive.org/details/bub_gb_u_T0u0IuuyIC.

Averroes, *Averrois in librum V (Δ) Metaphysicorum Aristotelis Commentarius*, ed. R. Ponzalli (Bern: Edizione Francke, 1971).

Averroes, *Commentarium Magnum in Aristotelis De Anima Libros*, ed. F. Stuart Crawford, Corpus Commentariorum Averrois in Aristotelem VI 1 (Cambridge, Mass.: The Mediaeval Academy of America, 1953).

Barth, E. M., *The Logic of the Articles in Traditional Philosophy: A Contribution to the Study of Conceptual Structures*, Eng. tr. E. M. Barth and T. C. Potts (Dordrecht: Reidel, 1974).

Boethius, A. M. S., *De Topicis Differentiis*, Eng. tr. Eleonore Stump (Ithaca: Cornell University Press, 1978).

Bradwardine, Thomas, *De Causa Dei contra Pelagium et de virtute causarum*, ed. Sir Henry Savile (London: Joannes Billius, 1618).

Bradwardine, Thomas, *Insolubilia*, ed. and Eng. tr. Stephen Read, Dallas Medieval Texts and Translations vol. 10 (Leuven: Peeters, 2010).

Brinkley, Richard, *Insolubilia*, in Paul Vincent Spade, *An Anonymous Fourteenth-Century Treatise on "Insolubles": Text and Study* (Licentiate Thesis, Pontifical Institute of Mediaeval Studies in Toronto, 1969), https://hdl.handle.net/2022/21929.

Brower, Jeffrey, 'Medieval Theories of Relations', *The Stanford Encyclopedia of Philosophy* (Winter 2018 Edition), ed. Edward N. Zalta, https://plato.stanford.edu/archives/win2018/entries/relations-medieval/.

Buridan, John, *Sophismata*, in *Summulae de practica sophismatum*, ed. Fabienne Pironet (Turnhout: Brepols, 2004); Eng. tr. in Buridan, *Summulae de Dialectica*, Eng. tr. Klima.

Buridan, John, *Summulae de Dialectica*, Eng. tr. Gyula Klima (New Haven: Yale University Press, 2001).

Buridan, John, *Treatise on Consequences*, Eng. tr. Stephen Read (New York: Fordham University Press, 2015), https://doi.org/10.5422/fordham/9780823257188.001.0001.

Burley, Walter, *De Obligationibus*, in R. Green, *An Introduction to the Logical Treatise De Obligationibus, With Critical Texts of William of Sherwood [?] and Walter Burley*, 2 vols (PhD thesis, Katholieke Universiteit Leuven, 1963), vol. II, pp. 34–96.

Burley, Walter, *De Puritate Artis Logicae*, ed. Philotheus Boehner (Saint Bonaventure: The Franciscan Institute, 1955); Eng. tr. Paul Vincent Spade, *On the Purity of the Art of Logic* (New Haven: Yale University Press, 2000).

Burley, Walter, *Insolubilia*, in Roure, 'La problématique des propositions insolubles', 262–84.

Burley, Walter, *Obligations*, (partially) tr. in Kretzmann and Stump, *The Cambridge Translations of Medieval Philosophical Texts*, vol. I, pp. 369–412.

Cohen, S. Marc and Reeve, C. D. C. 'Aristotle's Metaphysics', *The Stanford Encyclopedia of Philosophy* (Winter 2021 Edition), ed. Edward N. Zalta, https://plato.stanford.edu/archives/win2021/entries/aristotle-metaphysics/.

Conti, Alessandro, 'Walter Burley', *The Stanford Encyclopedia of Philosophy* (Summer 2016 Edition), ed. Edward N. Zalta, https://plato.stanford.edu/archives/sum2016/entries/burley/.

De Rijk, L. M., *Logica Modernorum: A Contribution to the History of Early Terminist Logic*, 3 vols. (Assen: Van Gorcum, 1962–67).

De Rijk, L. M., 'Some Notes on the Mediaeval Tract *De insolubilibus*, with the Edition of a Tract Dating from the end of the Twelfth Century', *Vivarium*, 4 (1966), 83–115.

De Rijk, L. M., 'The Development of Suppositio Naturalis in Medieval Logic', *Vivarium*, 9 (1971), 71–107.

Dumbleton, John, *Summa Logicae: Insolubilia*, ed. and Eng. tr. Barbara Bartocci and Stephen Read, in preparation.

Dutilh Novaes, Catarina, 'Form and Matter in Later Latin Medieval Logic: The Cases of *suppositio* and *consequentia*', *Journal of History of Philosophy*, 50 (2012), 339–64.

Emden, A. B., *A Biographical Register of the University of Oxford to A.D. 1500*, 3 vols (Oxford: Clarendon Press, 1957–59).

Gelber, Hester, 'The Fallacy of Accident and the "dictum de omni": Late Medieval Controversy over a Reciprocal Pair', *Vivarium*, 25 (1987), 110–45.

Hamesse, Jacqueline (ed.), *Les Auctoritates Aristotelis: un florilège médiéval. Étude historique et édition critique* (Louvain: Publications universitaires, 1974).

Heytesbury, William, 'The Verbs "Know" and "Doubt"', Eng. tr. in Kretzmann and Stump, *The Cambridge Translations of Medieval Philosophical Texts*, vol. I, pp. 435–79, https://doi.org/10.1017/cbo9781139171557.016.

Kilvington, Richard, *Quaestiones super libros Ethicorum*, ed. Monika Michalowska (Leiden: Brill, 2016), https://doi.org/10.1163/9789004331556.

Kilvington, Richard, *The Sophismata of Richard Kilvington*, ed. and Eng. tr. Barbara Kretzmann and Norman Kretzmann (Cambridge: Cambridge University Press, 1990).

Klima, Gyula, 'Existence and Reference in Medieval Logic', in *New Essays in Free Logic*, ed. A. Hieke and E. Morscher (Dordrecht: Springer 2001), pp. 197–226, https://doi.org/10.1007/978-94-015-9761-6_10.

Kneale, William, 'Aristotle and the *Consequentia Mirabilis*', *The Journal of Hellenic Studies*, 77 (1957), 62–66.

Kretzmann, Norman and Stump, Eleonore (ed. and tr.), *The Cambridge Translations of Medieval Philosophical Texts*, vol. I: *Logic and the Philosophy of Language* (Cambridge: Cambridge University Press, 1988), https://doi.org/10.1017/cbo9781139171557.

Latham, R. E., Howlett, D. R. and Ashdowne, R. K., *Dictionary of Medieval Latin from British Sources* (London: Oxford University Press for The British Academy, 1975–2013). See also https://logeion.uchicago.edu/lexidium.

Lindberg, David C., *Theories of Vision from Al-Kindi to Kepler* (Chicago: University of Chicago Press, 1976).

Longeway, John, 'Medieval Theories of Demonstration', *The Stanford Encyclopedia of Philosophy* (Spring 2021 Edition), ed. Edward N. Zalta, https://plato.stanford.edu/archives/spr2021/entries/demonstration-medieval/.

Maierù, Alfonso, 'Le ms. Oxford Canonici misc. 219 et la "Logica" de Strode', in *English Logic in Italy in the 14th and 15th centuries. Acts of the 5th European Symposium on Medieval Logic and Semantics, Rome, 10–14 November 1980*, ed. A. Maierù (Naples: Bibliopolis, 1982), pp. 87–110.

Manlevelt, Thomas, *Quaestiones libri Porphyrii*, ed. Alfred van der Helm (Leiden: Brill, 2014), https://doi.org/10.1163/9789004264304.

Murdoch, John. 'From Social into Intellectual Factors: an Aspect of the Unitary Character of Late Medieval Learning', in *The Cultural Context of Medieval Learning*, ed. John E. Murdoch and Edith D. Sylla (Dordrecht: Reidel, 1975), 271–339.

Nuchelmans, G., 'The Distinction *actus exercitus/actus significatus* in Medieval Semantics', in *Meaning and Inference in Medieval Philosophy*, ed. Norman Kretzmann (Dordrecht: Kluwer, 1988), pp. 57–90.

Ockham, Guillelmus de, *Expositio super libros Elenchorum*, ed. Francesco Del Punta, Opera Philosophica III (St Bonaventure: The Franciscan Institute, 1979).

Ockham, Guillelmus de, *Summa Logicae*, ed. Philotheus Boehner, Gedeon Gál, and Stephen Brown, Opera philosophica I (St Bonaventure: The Franciscan Institute, 1974).

Ottman, J. and Wood, R., 'Walter of Burley: His Life and Works', *Vivarium*, 37 (1999), 1–23.

Parsons, Terence, *Articulating Medieval Logic* (New York: Fordham University Press, 2014).

Parsons, Terence, 'The Power of Medieval Logic', in *Later Medieval Metaphysics: Ontology, Language and Logic*, ed. C. Bolyard and R. Keele (Oxford: Oxford University Press, 2013), pp. 188–205.

Paul of Venice, *Logica Magna* (Venice: Albertinus Vercellensis, 1499).

Paul of Venice, *Logica Magna, Prima Pars: Tractatus de Terminis*, ed. and Eng. tr. Norman Kretzmann (Oxford: Oxford University Press for the British Academy, 1979).

Paul of Venice, *Logica Magna, Prima Pars: Tractatus de Scire et Dubitare*, ed. and Eng. tr. Patricia Clarke (Oxford: Oxford University Press for the British Academy, 1981).

Paul of Venice, *Logica Magna, Secunda Pars: Capitula de Conditionali et de Rationali*, ed. and Eng. tr. George E. Hughes (Oxford: Oxford University Press for the British Academy, 1990).

Paul of Venice, *Logica Magna, Secunda Pars: Tractatus de Obligationibus*, ed. and Eng. tr. E. Jennifer Ashworth (Oxford: Oxford University Press for the British Academy, 1988).

Paul of Venice, *Logica Magna: The Treatise on Insolubles*, ed. and Eng. tr. Barbara Bartocci and Stephen Read, Dallas Medieval Texts and Translations, vol. 25 (Leuven: Peeters, 2022), https://doi.org/10.2307/jj.890665.

Peter of Spain, *Summaries of Logic*, ed. Brian Copenhaver (Oxford: Oxford University Press, 2013).

Pironet, Fabienne, *Guillaume Heytesbury: Sophismata Asinina* (Paris: Vrin, 1994).

Pozzi, Lorenzo, *Il Mentitore e il Medioevo: il Dibattito sui Paradossi dell'Autoriferimento. Scelta di Testi, Commento, Traduzione* (Parma: Edizioni Zara, 1987).

Read, Stephen, '*Descensus copulatim*: Albert of Saxony and Thomas Maulfelt', *Itinéraires d'Albert de Saxe: Paris-Vienne au XIVe*, ed. J. Biard (Paris: Vrin, 1991), pp. 71–85.

Read, Stephen, 'Inferences', *The Cambridge History of Medieval Philosophy*, ed. R. Pasnau, 2 vols (Cambridge, Cambridge University Press, 2010), vol. I, pp. 173–84, https://doi.org/10.1017/chol9780521762168.015.

Read, Stephen, 'Logic in the Latin West in the Fourteenth Century', in *The Cambridge Companion to Medieval Logic*, ed. Catarina Dutilh Novaes and Stephen Read (Cambridge: Cambridge University Press, 2016), pp. 142–65, https://doi.org/10.1017/CBO9781107449862.007.

Read, Stephen, 'Medieval Theories of Properties of Terms', *The Stanford Encyclopedia of Philosophy* (Spring 2023 Edition), ed. Edward N. Zalta and Uri Nodelman, https://plato.stanford.edu/archives/spr2023/entries/medieval-terms/.

Read, Stephen, 'The Calculators and the Insolubles: Bradwardine, Kilvington, Heytesbury, Swyneshed and Dumbleton', in *Quantifying Aristotle: the Impact, Spread and Decline of the 'Calculatores' Tradition*, ed. Edith D. Sylla and Daniel A. Di Liscia (Leiden: Brill, 2022), pp. 126–52, https://doi.org/10.1163/9789004512054_007.

Read, Stephen, 'Theories of Paradox from Thomas Bradwardine to Paul of Venice', in *Theories of Paradox in the Middle Ages*, ed. Stephen Read and Barbara Bartocci, pp. 11–42.

Read, Stephen, 'Thomas of Cleves and Collective Supposition', *Vivarium*, 29 (1991), 50–84.

Read, Stephen, 'Truth, Signification and Paradox', in *Unifying the Philosophy of Truth*, ed. T. Achourioti, H. Galinon, J. Martinez Fernández and K. Fujimoto, (Dordrecht: Springer, 2015), pp. 393–408, https://doi.org/10.1007/978-94-017-9673-6.

Read, Stephen, 'Walter Segrave's "Insolubles": A Restrictivist Response to Bradwardine', in *Theories of Paradox in the Middle Ages*, ed. Stephen Read and Barbara Bartocci, pp. 43–66.

Read, Stephen and Bartocci, Barbara (eds), *Theories of Paradox in the Middle Ages* (London: College Publications, 2023).

Roure, M.-L., 'La problématique des propositions insolubles au XIIIe siècle et au début du XIVe, suivie de l'édition des traités de W.Shyreswood, W. Burleigh et Th. Bradwardine', *Archives d'histoire doctrinale et littéraire du moyen âge*, 36–37 (1970), 205–326.

Schum, Wilhelm, *Beschreibendes Verzeichniss der Amplonianischen Handschriften-Sammlung zu Erfurt* (Berlin: Weidemannsche Buchhandlung, 1887).

Scotus, John Duns, *Quaestiones super Librum Elenchorum*, in *Opera Philosophica* vol. II, ed. R. Andrews, O. Bychkov, S. Ebbesen, G. Etzkorn, G. Gál, R. Green, T. Noone, R. Plevano and A. Traver (St. Bonaventure: Franciscan Institute; Washington, DC: Catholic University of America, 2004).

Scotus, John Duns, *Super libros Elenchorum*, in *Opera omnia* vol. II, ed. L. Vivès (Paris: Bibliopolam Editorem via vulgo dicta Delambre, 1891).

Segrave, Charles W., *The Segrave Family 1066–1935* (London: Novello, 1936).

Spade, Paul Vincent, *The Mediaeval Liar: A Catalogue of the* Insolubilia-*Literature* (Toronto: The Pontifical Institute of Mediaeval Studies, 1975)

Spade, Paul Vincent and Read, Stephen, 'Insolubles', *The Stanford Encyclopedia of Philosophy* (Winter 2021 Edition), ed. Edward N. Zalta, https://plato.stanford.edu/archives/win2021/entries/insolubles/.

Synan, Edward A., 'The *Insolubilia* of Roger Nottingham, O.F.M.', *Mediaeval Studies*, 26 (1964), 257–70.

Uguccione de Pisa, *Derivationes*, ed. Enzo Cecchini et al., 2 vols (Florence: SISMEL. Edizioni del Galluzzo, 2004).

About the Team

Alessandra Tosi was the managing editor for this book.

Magdalena Bieniak, Peter King, and Cecilia Trifogli refereed the manuscript for the Medieval Text Consortium.

Adèle Kreager proofread the book.

Peter Hartman converted the initial Word document into LaTeX.

Chris Martin designed the book's layout.

Jan Maliszewski implemented the parallel typesetting with reledmac/reledpar packages.

This volume uses the Tex Gyre Pagella font family.

Jeevanjot Kaur Nagpal designed the cover of this book. The cover was produced in InDesign using Fontin and Calibri fonts.

www.ingramcontent.com/pod-product-compliance
Lightning Source LLC
Chambersburg PA
CBHW050244170426
43202CB00015B/2907